COFFEE
with a
COFFIN

COFFEE
with a
COFFIN

Permanent Lessons from
the Impermanence of Life

ALOK RANJAN

Hay House Publishers India
Australia • India
United Kingdom • United States

Hay House Publishers (India) Pvt. Ltd.
Muskaan Complex, Plot No.3, B-2 Vasant Kunj, New Delhi-110 070, India
Hay House Inc., PO Box 5100, Carlsbad, CA 92018-5100, USA
Hay House UK, Ltd., The Sixth Floor, Watson House, 54 Baker Street, W1U 7BU, UK
Hay House Australia Pty Ltd., 18/36 Ralph St., Alexandria NSW 2015, Australia

Email: contact@hayhouse.co.in
www.hayhouse.co.in

Illustrations used in this book have been sketched
and provided by the author.

ISBN 978-93-91067-48-9
ISBN 978-93-91067-78-6 (ebook)

Printed at Repro India Limited

To the river Ganga which gave me
the most insightful experience of life.

Contents

Introduction 11

Part 1
Death Is Not Our Enemy

Chapter 1
How We Ignore the Biggest Reality of Life 17

Chapter 2
The Enemy Is a Friend in Disguise 29

Chapter 3
We Don't Have to Wait for a Crisis 37

Part 2
How to Develop Awareness of Death

Chapter 4
Let's Go to Our Own Funeral 45

Chapter 5
Let's Make a Trip to the Greatest University in
the World 51

Chapter 6
Let's Turn Those Spare Minutes into Seeds of
Enlightenment 57

Chapter 7
Let's Write Today What We Are Supposed to
Write in the End   61

Chapter 8
When We Lose a Loved One, We Shouldn't
Lose the Lesson   65

Chapter 9
If We Want the Message, Everybody Can
Be a Messenger   71

Chapter 10
The Journey Will Be Better If We Find a Co-traveller   75

Part 3
The Benefits of the Awareness of Death

Chapter 11
Finding Out What We Truly Want   81

Chapter 12
The Courage to Live the Life We Want to Live   87

Chapter 13
Mental Peace and Loss of Fear   93

Chapter 14
A Strong Purpose and Undefeatable Spirit in Life   99

Chapter 15
More Compassion, Less Grudges   103

Chapter 16
Rise of the Creative Giant Sleeping inside Us   107

Contents

Chapter 17
Knowledge of What Truly Matters in Life   111

Chapter 18
The Urge to Leave Something behind Before We Leave   115

Chapter 19
A Stronger Desire to Impress Ourselves   121

Chapter 20
Feeling Closer to Our Loved Ones   125

Chapter 21
Being a Great Friend to People on Deathbed   131

Chapter 22
Humility In, Ego Out   137

Chapter 23
No More Procrastination   143

Chapter 24
Living in the NOW   147

Chapter 25
Saying 'Thanks' More   151

Chapter 26
A Life with Fewer Attachments and More Freedom   155

Chapter 27
Discovering the Delivery Date of Happiness   163

Chapter 28
Awakening of a Great Desire to Find the Truth   169

CONTENTS

Part 4
Tools

I.	Build a New Way of Thinking	177
II.	Visualise Your Cremation	185
III.	Visit a Cremation Ground	187
IV.	One-Minute Awareness Pills	189
V.	Remember the Loved Ones You Have Lost	191
VI.	Learn from Stranger Teachers	193
VII.	Find Some Co-Travellers	195
VIII.	Build a Mental Monastery	197
IX.	Write Your Will	199
X.	Find Out the Most Important Things	201
XI.	Write Your Obituary	203
XII.	Help the Dying with Listening and Tonglen Meditation	205
XIII.	Be Totally Present	209
XIV.	Watch Your Breath	211

Conclusion — 219

My Story: Yesterday Death Kissed Me and Then Ditched Me — 223

Recommended Readings — 231

Acknowledgements — 233

INTRODUCTION

*C*ricket is one of the most popular games on this planet. Around 2.5 billion people either love playing it or enjoy watching it. On a similar note, staying alive is the most popular desire in the world. One of the primary goals of more than 7 billion human beings is to keep living on this earth as long as possible. And there is a strange similarity between one of the most popular games on the planet and the most popular desire in the world.

In cricket, there is a batsman who is surrounded by eleven alert and seasoned players whose sole aim is to get him out of the game. These eleven players pose multiple threats to the batsman. The bowlers in the game will throw the ball at the batsman, and if he fails to hit it with his bat and the ball ends up hitting the wickets, our dear batsman will be called bowled and he will be dismissed. If the batsman hits the ball with his bat or gloves and the ball is caught by any of the opposition players before touching the ground, the batsman will be caught out and his game will end. If the batsman steps out of the crease and the wicket-keeper hits the stumps with the ball, the batsman will be stumped and he will have to leave the ground. The batsman can also be given an LBW (leg before wicket) in the case where the ball, which was supposedly hitting the wickets, gets blocked by the batsman's body or any equipment other than the bat or gloves. Also, if the batsman is running between wickets and any of the fielders hits the stumps with the ball, he will be given a run out. But that's not all; if the batsman hits the stumps with his body or any sports equipment while attempting to play a shot, he will be considered hit-wicket.

In all of these cases, his game will end and he won't be able to stay on the pitch or come back to it again no matter how much he tries, pleads, or threatens. If his game is over, frankly speaking, it's over. He has to work really hard to save himself every minute, and yet he can fail.

When it comes to the struggle to stay alive, the condition of human life is not much different from that of the batsman. Every day we come across so many things which can take our lives. We can catch a deadly disease. A tiny mosquito or an invisible virus can stop our bodily functions and end our life. We can meet with an accident both on the street as well as in the air. We can get murdered by some criminal or lunatic. And if you think we are safe in our houses, you can't be further from the truth. We can die by drowning in the bathtub or falling from the bed. Our lives can also end while we are sitting at home, sipping tea, and discussing the latest movie with our family members. In 2020, an aeroplane fell down in a housing society in Karachi, Pakistan, and people living in those houses were killed immediately along with the travellers and the pilots.

Apart from these external causes, there are many internal factors as well, such as depression and anxiety, that can speed up our death. Even if somehow, we are able to save ourselves from all these countless life-threatening scenarios, old age is definitely going to kill us after a while. In short, no doctor, no hospital, and no security guards can protect us from this ultimate cause of death.

In other words, we are like that batsman who needs to be mindful of all the looming threats to life. Every moment carries the potential of annihilation, and yet we have to survive. That's the great similarity between the game of cricket and the desire to stay alive. And if we use this similarity as a launch pad to inquire deeper into the mindset of the batsman, we can open the doors to a new kind of life.

In the game of cricket, the batsman is always alert about all the threats to his survival in the game. He doesn't ignore them. He doesn't deny them. On the contrary, he faces this bitter truth and prepares himself to handle it. He uses this threat to enhance his performance, to show his best in the game, and to make a mark in the world of sports. He also knows that even if he plays very skilfully, the game will be over after a while and he will have to return to his home. He doesn't fool himself with the notion that the game will keep going on forever. His aim is to perform his best in whatever time is given to him and to leave the pitch with pride in his eyes and satisfaction in his heart when the game ends.

We can have the same approach towards our desire to stay alive. We can stop assuming that we will keep living on the earth forever. We can accept the threat of death and use it to maximise our happiness, love, meaningfulness, and creativity in life. We can be the batsman in the playground of life who impresses himself and others with his performance and gets the maximum satisfaction out of the game.

Many of you might still feel that this logic sounds strange. After all, we are supposed to be afraid of death and should protect ourselves from it. But we will ignore this approach for a while and experiment with a different perspective in the coming days. With this book, we will find out how we can use death to live a better life. We will see how the poison of life can be turned into the alchemy of life. We will explore the possibility of using the ultimate sleep as a motivational factor to wake up now.

But it's not going to be an easy and smooth journey. We are going to change our entire approach towards death step by step. We are going to confront our deepest fear and transform it into a great strength. In a world where almost everybody seems to believe that they are not going to die, we are going to focus on the fact that we are not immortals.

As the author of this book and your co-traveller, I will be sharing my thoughts, experiences, and learning with you on this subject. I will be using stories from my own life and popular stories from the public domain to express my perspective. I hope you will enjoy this little journey which has the potential to give a new direction to your life.

As the first step of this journey, we need to understand our unpleasant relationship with this friend who has been misunderstood as an enemy since our birth. So, let me start by sharing a strange experience I had while visiting a place during holidays. It was not a very pleasant place and most of the people would avoid going there at any cost. But I had made my mind to be there to learn something which no other place on the earth could teach.

Part 1

DEATH IS NOT OUR ENEMY

"It is not death that a man should fear, but he should fear never beginning to live."
— Marcus Aurelius

Chapter 1

HOW WE IGNORE THE
BIGGEST REALITY OF LIFE

"A man begins dying at the moment of his birth. Most people live in denial of Death's patient courtship until, late in life and deep in sickness, they become aware of him sitting bedside."

— Dean Koontz, *The Husband*

Nigambodh Ghat is thousands of years old. If you go there anytime during the day, you will always find it crowded with people, and there is a reason behind it. After all, it's one of the largest cremation grounds of the second most populated country in the world. And it's also the place which has given me a unique insight about human psychology.

Most of the people who live in Delhi or in the area around it will surely visit it at least once. The irony is that most of them won't visit this place out of their own choice nor they would visit it walking on their feet. My case was different. I had deliberately made a choice to be there. I had decided to visit this place on one of my weekends. I wanted to experience how death looked like. I wanted to breathe the air which was filled with the smoke coming out from the burning dead bodies. I wanted to see this place at least once with my open eyes before I might have to visit it with my eyes closed forever.

Contrary to my expectations, the place was filled with an ethereal calmness and soothing silence. The place was very well-organised and it had the capacity to burn more than one hundred dead bodies at the same time. If the god of death, Yama, went on a rampage, he won't have to worry about the disposal of the lifeless bodies. It had many concrete platforms, and each platform was built to burn one corpse. There were at least half-a-dozen wooden funeral pyres here and there which had been burning for some time. Some of the dead bodies had been completely burnt, and I could see heaps of ashes and some half-burnt wooden pieces in their places.

A human body is a wonderful creation of nature. We have lived with it so long yet we don't know what kind of things it contains. If an adult body's blood vessels are laid end to end, they will be so long that they can circle earth's equator four times. Our nerves are super-efficient at carrying signals. Information zooms through them at the speed of four hundred kilometres per hour. Our lungs contain almost 1,500 miles of airways and an average human being breathes in around 11,000 litres of air every day. Our heart beats around 100,000 times a day, 365,000,000 times a year, and 2.5 billion times in an average life span. In one year, a human heart would pump enough blood to fill an Olympic size pool. An average-sized human being eats about 33 tons of food in his lifetime, which is about the weight of six elephants. The average person produces enough saliva in their lifetime to fill two average-sized swimming pools. An adult body is made up of around 7 octillion atoms.

These are just some of the things that the human body contains. And apart from these tangible elements, an average human body carries millions of thoughts, experiences, loads of knowledge, hundreds of emotions, the memory of countless events, and the potential to do unimaginable things. It was humbling to see how a little fire could convert this treasure of amazing things into a bucket of worthless ash within an hour.

As I was walking around, I saw a river passing by the cremation ground. Nigambodh Ghat is situated on the bank of river Yamuna. Hindus have a tradition of burning dead bodies on the bank of a holy river because they believe that it helps in the afterlife of the deceased person. I stepped ahead and reached the bank of the river. There was a fresh dead body lying on a pile of wooden blocks. It was wrapped in a deep yellow cloth. A little bit of the face was visible and I could see the closed eyes. The person had left the world just a few hours ago, perhaps. Around fifty people had come to see off the dead man. They were sitting on a big platform near the funeral pyre. They must have been his friends, relatives, and acquaintances. I went and sat with them in a corner. Nobody smiled at me. Nobody asked about my identity. They must have thought that I was one of the acquaintances of the dead man who had come to pay homage. After all, it was a funeral and not a wedding ceremony where many people would like to come happily.

I sat with them with a silent mind and started observing the rituals being performed at the pyre. You can imagine the feel of that place. It was one of the busiest cremation grounds in the world. There were at least a dozen dead bodies around us. There was one dead body in front of us, waiting for the fire which would remove its every trace on the earth in the coming hour. Millions of people had turned into ashes here in its history of thousands of years. This place had the presence of death in every dust particle there.

Then I overheard some of the words which were being spoken by the people sitting near me. They were casually discussing which credit card would be better for shopping in malls. One of them was counting the benefits of the card he was using. Another person was suggesting him to try another card that offered a better credit score and lower interest rate. I then heard more from the conversation taking place around me. Somebody was discussing some superhit Hindi movie which had released that month and this person was sharing his disappointment with the acting of his favourite star. He was also sharing his point of view about what kind of movies that star should take up and how he should improve his acting skills to make better movies. Finally, I heard one person talking about the dead man lying in front of us. He was talking about how much money and property the gentleman might have left for his family members. Then he talked about the last death ceremony he had attended and the kind of food that was served in that ceremony. He didn't seem to be very happy with the quality of food that time and hoped that he would have a better experience this time.

It was my first visit to a cremation ground, and I couldn't believe what I was hearing. I had expected that the environment of a cremation ground will remind people of their own mortality and make them silently think about their own lives. But no, these people were chatting as if they were sitting in a roadside café.

It has been years since that experience. I have visited Nigambodh Ghat many times in this duration. I have also been to some funerals. The only difference is that now I don't get surprised when I see people talking about mundane things and doing their best to ignore the topic of death even if they are sitting face to face with it. Sometimes I feel there is a silent universal conspiracy to hide the topic of death so that it doesn't bother us and doesn't disrupt our dreams for the future as it makes us ignore the possibility of losing everything in a fraction of a moment.

And if we think that the world was different thousands of years ago and people thought differently when they were riding horses and using bows and arrows, we are mistaken. At around 3,000 BC, five brothers had lost their kingdom in India and were exiled for twelve years into forests because they had been defeated by their cousin brothers in a game of gambling. While they were roaming around on the tough terrains of a jungle, they felt extremely thirsty. They decided to take rest under a tree, and the youngest brother went ahead in search of water. Very soon, he found a beautiful lake with crystal clear water which was being guarded by a yaksha, a type of ancient god. The yaksha said that he had no issues with the thirsty man drinking the water, but he would have to give answers to his questions before he had his first sip. The youngest brother ignored his warning and drank the water. He fainted and fell unconscious within a second. One by one, three more brothers came to the beautiful lake, ignored the yaksha's warning and met with the same fate. Then the eldest one came to the lake and saw his apparently lifeless brothers lying on its bank. He had enough sense to take the yaksha's warning seriously and decided to give answers to his cryptic questions.

The yaksha asked many questions and one of them was, "What's the biggest surprise on this earth?"

The eldest brother replied with a serious face, "Every day, many people are going to the abode of death. Yet others think they are going to live forever. What can be a bigger surprise than that?" The yaksha was pleased with his answers. He gave him permission to drink the water and breathed life into the bodies of his four brothers.

Human beings have been dying for thousands of years, yet they have been ignoring and denying this ultimate final reality of life. And who knows, they might continue doing this for the coming thousands of years as well.

Death will embrace all of us sooner or later but we will avoid touching this subject again and again.

And we are very creative when it comes to finding ways to ignore this subject not only in conversations but also in silent times of contemplation.

If the yaksha had asked the same question today, he would have got the same answer. Actually, nowadays we have figured out even better ways to ignore this bitter and ultimate reality of human life. We have created more and more distractions so that we can turn a blind eye to what's in store for us and focus more on pursuing sensual pleasures, never-ending entertainment, and random hobbies to forget the inner fear.

And we have a very strong reason to ignore this fear and hide it under the blankets of distractions. The reason behind it is simple: death is the end of everything we know in our life. Our family, friends, money, possessions, career, thoughts, feelings, body—everything we have accumulated and enjoyed in this life goes away in a second and they go away forever. No force in the world can bring any of them back, not even for a moment.

We come face to face with this reality when we see the death of a loved one. When we see their lifeless body, we realise that one cannot take away even a thread with himself after his demise. That person cannot hear us, touch us, play with us, or fight with us anymore. Every moment we spent with that person becomes a part of some painful or nostalgic memory. And if the death is unexpected, we don't even get a chance to say goodbye or give them a final hug. We also realise the same thing will happen to us one day. Our body will be lying without any life in front of others, and we won't be able to see them, talk to them, and touch them again. This thought makes us shudder with fear.

No power in the world has been able to prevent somebody from dying. Medical sciences can postpone death with the help of their wonderful medicines and equipment, but they cannot stop it from happening in future. Deep inside, we all realise how helpless we are in front of the claws of death. Even the richest and most powerful ones have to die one day, and their unlimited money and power cannot make them stay on the earth even for a minute longer if their time has come.

So, what do we do? We start building a psychological defence system based on lies. We start convincing ourselves that death will come to others, not to us. We start telling ourselves that nothing will happen to us. We hope that some medicine or miracle cure will be discovered before our expected death that can stop us from dying. So, we start making long-term plans for the upcoming decades of our lives. We create wonderful dreams about our future and fall in love with them. The possibility of death rarely crops up either in our plans or in our dreams.

We start hiding the signs of ageing because every white or lost hair and every wrinkle on the face reminds us of being closer to death. We start dyeing our hair, we start using cosmetics to hide our wrinkles, we start trying to act like younger people, and we also start giving wrong information about our age while talking to others. Some of us go to the extreme end and end up destroying our face with plastic surgery. We feel extremely elated when somebody tells us that we look young and feel immense pain when somebody says that we are getting old. We avoid every conversation about death or if we can't avoid it, we try to keep it as short as possible. We can spend hours and hours discussing the score sheets of popular sports personalities, watching mindless TV shows, discussing the private lives of our colleagues, exploring cool hobbies, and finding out where we can find the best coffee in the city, but we cannot find even a single hour in a year to contemplate and have a discussion about death. And if somebody dares to bring this topic in a conversation, we shut that person down by saying that we shouldn't focus on negative things of life and instead, we should focus on living and enjoying our life. We give this kind of logic.

When somebody dies, many of us try to remove each and everything which reminds us of that person. We talk about that person as little as possible. We believe in moving on and we decide to stop living in the past. This act of moving on is motivated by the fact that the demise of that person somewhere reminds us of what's going to happen to us as well.

Many people turn to religion for solace. Religions tell us that there is an infinite afterlife waiting for us after the death of our physical body. We never try to check if their sayings are true or not. We blindly believe them because our belief works as anaesthesia and temporarily stops us from feeling inner agony and terror. We develop sugar-coated personal philosophies and create random life goals to keep ourselves busy so that we don't get time to look within and face our inner demons. We tell ourselves that we cannot stop living just because death has to come one day. And what's our definition of living? It's keeping ourselves occupied with goals like having real estate properties, getting new tiles in our bathroom, discussing the politics of some faraway country we have nothing to do with, learning new ways of making pasta, and torturing others with the unending stories of our achievements.

I DON'T HAVE THE TIME
TO THINK ABOUT DEATH.
I'M BUSY CHECKING THE
VACATION PICTURES OF
MY FAVOURITE CELEB.

Life gives us enough opportunities to leave our escapist attitude and face the inner fear of death. When we lose a loved one, we come to see the capacity of death. When we have a close brush with death, we see how close we could have been to losing everything. When we read about hundreds of people losing their lives in accidents or violence or a natural calamity, we again get a chance to face the fierceness of death. But we are the masters of the art of escapism. Even those patients who are on their deathbed cannot stay away from this tempting habit of escaping from the reality. They keep hoping to hear the 'good news' that a new medicine has been invented which will make sure that they will live for many more years. We try to behave like ostriches by burying our heads in the sands of escapism and distractions. But history tells us that this technique has never been able to safeguard any ostrich.

But then we ask, what's the point in talking or thinking about death if we cannot do much about it? That's a very good question. If death has to come, it will come. We cannot stop it from coming. It's something totally beyond our control. Won't it be better if we focus on what's in our hand? Isn't it more sensible to focus on our life and enjoy it as much as possible before it's taken away from our hands? That's true. We cannot stop death from coming. It will come to us whenever it has decided to come irrespective of the precautions we take in our lives. But there is one thing we can do. We can change our relationship with death. We can stop ignoring it. We can go and meet it before it comes to meet us.

No, I am not talking about ending our life. By doing that, we would be committing a heinous crime against our body and soul. I am talking about developing another kind of relationship with death. It's the kind of relationship that will enhance the quality of our life and fill it with more meaningfulness, satisfaction, success, and happiness. You might think that this is impossible but the truth is that it's very much possible. Countless people in the history of humankind have proved with their own lives that it's possible and it's practical to have an amicable relationship with death.

So, let's take a new direction and start a new journey with the foe who can become a friend, with the terror which can become a teacher, with the end which can become a beginning. We just need a little courage for this journey and we all have that courage.

Chapter 2

THE ENEMY IS A
FRIEND IN DISGUISE

"If you have a strong sense of the certainty of death and of the uncertainty of its arrival, you will be motivated from within. It will be as if a friend is cautioning, 'Be careful, be earnest, another day is passing.'"

— Dalai Lama,
Advice on Dying: And Living a Better Life

*O*nce upon a time, a Samurai warrior went to meet a Zen monk. The Samurai had a question in his mind which was making him restless. He thought only a wise person like the monk could answer his question. After reaching the destination, the Samurai bowed down to the monk and asked, "Sir, can you please tell me the difference between hell and heaven?"

The monk looked at him with a clear sarcasm in his eyes and replied, "Only an idiot like you can ask such foolish questions."

The Samurai was taken aback by the answer. His face turned red with anger. He pulled out his sword and roared, "How dare you talk to me like this?"

The monk showed no sign of fear or worry on his face and then spoke calmly, "Right now you are in hell."

The Samurai got conscious of what he was doing. He understood the monk had deliberately given that answer to offend him. His hand stopped, his face lost a bit of fury, and he felt stillness in his mind and body. The monk, who was observing him like a mother observes her erratic child, spoke with a compassionate smile, "Right now you are in heaven." The Samurai understood what the monk wanted to tell him. He bowed down again, put his sword into the scaffold, and left with slow steps.

So, what was the thing that changed and brought the Samurai from hell into heaven? His circumstances hadn't changed and he was not offered any apology by the monk to make him feel better. Only one thing had changed—he had become aware of his anger. As soon as he became aware of his anger, he started feeling peace and tranquillity. Anger lost its grip on him, and he was no longer tormented by it.

Awareness is the magical element that can transform anything into something good. When a mother is aware of her child's needs, she knows how to take care of him. When we are aware of impending dangers, we know how to protect ourselves from them. When we are aware of our emotions, we know how to manage them well. Death or the fear of it is no exception. Add the element of awareness to it and we will see it change from a foe to a friend.

So far, we have been ignoring death and hiding it underneath the piles of distractions so much that it has gone into the deepest recesses of our mind. We have almost convinced ourselves to forget about it and believe that it won't come into our own lives or maybe it will come to us after a very long time and thus we don't need to be concerned about it. But the bitter truth is that death doesn't start ignoring us just because we start ignoring it. When it decides to meet us, it won't worry about the treatment it's going to get from us. It's much like those loan recovery agents who will be at our doors whether we like it or not.

To understand it better, let's take a look around in the world. Let's read a bit of news and history. Then we will find that there is no pattern about when and how death comes into anybody's life. Even the most powerful and secure people lost their lives when death decided to embrace them. Julius Caesar was a great king and ruled one of the biggest empires of the world. He was assassinated in his court by his own people. John F. Kennedy was the most powerful leader of the most powerful country on the earth. He was shot in his head in front of thousands of people while he was being guarded by the best police and army in the world. Indira Gandhi was the prime minister of the world's largest democracy. She was shot by her own bodyguards in the most secure house of the country, the prime ministerial residence. These examples tell us that there is nothing called absolute security in the world. There is no force in the universe which can guarantee flawless protection from death. We may spend every minute of our life in trying to make ourselves secure, but we cannot be completely certain about our safety.

This reminds me of a wonderful story I had read during my childhood. Once upon a time, an astrologer came to the court of a king. The astrologer was among the best in his field, and his prophecies never went wrong. Whatever he said came true eventually. His words were so accurate that people felt he could see the future with a telescope. The king was very curious about his future. He showed his horoscope to the astrologer and requested him to make some predictions about his life and fortune. Like most of the kings, he too was very ambitious about the expansion of his

empire and power. He was hoping to hear some wonderful things from the man who never said anything wrong.

The astrologer studied the horoscope carefully and then spoke with a grave voice, "Your majesty! Tomorrow evening you will die." The king got so shocked after hearing this that he almost fell from his throne. His dreams of becoming a richer and stronger king got a major jolt and his face turned red. He asked the astrologer if he was sure about the correctness of his findings. The astrologer said he would never give such sad news without being absolutely sure about it. The king asked him if anything could be done to change the future. The astrologer said that his job was only to give information about the future milestones on the path of life, and it was not possible for him to change the milestones or the direction of the path. In today's language, the astrologer was like Google Maps. It will tell you about the path you have taken and if you don't like what Google Maps tells you, you cannot ask it to change the details of the path.

The king couldn't sleep the whole night. His previous nights used to be full of golden dreams of a promising future but on that fateful day, his dreams were full of fear and uncertainty. He tried to convince himself that the astrologer could be wrong, but deep in his heart, he knew that the astrologer's reputation for honesty and the mastery over his subject was lily-white.

The king couldn't guess from where the death would come to him. Maybe his ministers had planned a coup and wanted to get him killed. Maybe his own queen was having an affair with some courtier and they had decided to poison his food. Maybe he would be killed by one of his sons since they were in a hurry to become the king. The king realised that he couldn't trust anybody. The astrologer could predict the time of death, but he couldn't give any information about the method of death.

The king made a quick decision which he had to implement if he had to save his life. In the early morning, he wore the dress of a farmer, put a fake beard on his face, took his sword and the fastest horse from the royal stable, and made a journey towards the borders of his kingdom. He let the horse choose its own direction. If the king himself didn't know where he was going, how could his potential assassin guess his movements? That was the logic he gave himself. The fear of death had transformed the man from an ambitious king to a scared absconder within a day. He kept riding his horse throughout the day and didn't make a single stop to drink water or have some food. These things could wait, he told himself. Staying alive was his prime concern.

In the late evening, when the darkness had started enveloping the sky, he finally stopped his dead tired horse. Now none of them had the energy to inch ahead. He saw a beautiful pond shining with clean water. He was thirsty and so was the horse. He got down and started drinking the water. The horse also followed him. After filling his belly with the water which tasted better than anything he had tasted in his entire royal life, he lied down on the green and soft grass. Now finally he was safe. Nobody knew where he was, and if nobody knew where he was, how could anybody kill him? He smiled thinking about this question. For the first time, the astrologer was going to be wrong. He had defeated his destiny, and he was going to live. He felt a surge of pride in his chest for his intelligence and determination.

Then a black shadow appeared and the king became alert. He had kept his sword away from himself due to carelessness. Before he could stand up and get his sword, he felt an axe at his neck. A tall and dark man was holding the axe. He spoke with a mocking smile on his face, "I admire your speed. I never believed you would be able to make this far in such a short time." And then he made the fatal blow. The astrologer was not wrong.

This is a metaphorical story. It doesn't mean that one must have complete faith in astrologers. It simply means that there is no place in the world that can guarantee absolute safety and we cannot do much about postponing our death if our time has come. So when we make security arrangements, death smirks. When we try to ignore our own mortality, death laughs. When we pretend that death doesn't exist, death giggles. It will come whenever it wants to. It doesn't need our invitation or permission. Our human life is always insecure and will always remain insecure. We all know this fact. But we try to forget it because of the fear and anxiety it invokes in us.

But maybe death is not as bad as it appears to be. Let's take a minute to imagine a world which has no death. A world where human beings, animals, birds, and trees have been getting older and weaker for thousands of years, but they cannot die. Their haplessness will increase day by day and there will be no respite from this misery. They would be doomed to stay alive forever, with their frail, diseased, and incredibly weak bodies. Also, there will be no place left for newborn babies. Would you like to live in such a world? Would you like to have immortality which promises nothing but misery and diseases and ageing bodies? Most of us won't welcome such a possibility.

Death is just a fact of life, like all other facts of life. Whether it turns out to be a monster or an angel largely depends upon how we look at it. If we are smart enough, we can use it to our own advantage. We can learn from it and use it to make our lives better, happier, full of love, more fulfilling, and prosperous. So far, we have been scared of it because we know it will steal away our lives and the lives of the people we love. But now let's try a different approach. Instead of being afraid of it and ignoring it and hiding and denying it, we will confront it. We will accept it and try to understand it. The key to all this lies in developing the awareness of death. If we figure out this element, we will open the possibilities for a new kind of life.

So how can we develop awareness of death? Do we have to go through a life-threatening experience or put ourselves in danger? Let's find out.

Chapter 3

WE DON'T HAVE TO WAIT
FOR A CRISIS

*"Normally we do not like to think about death.
We would rather think about life. Why reflect
on death? When you start preparing for death
you soon realise that you must look into your
life now . . . and come to face the truth of your
self. Death is like a mirror in which the true
meaning of life is reflected."*

— Sogyal Rinpoche, *The Tibetan Book of
Living and Dying*

Two years ago, I had gone to a hospital because a friend of mine was expecting a child. While I was sitting in the reception hall, waiting for the good news, I saw something which still makes me wonder about an interesting quality of human life.

I saw a couple coming out of the interior of the hospital with a newly born baby. That baby was wrapped in a blanket, her eyes were closed and she was in a deep sleep. The couple looked extremely happy and excited. They had a few people with them who were probably their relatives, and their happiness also showed on their faces. They crossed an extremely old woman sitting in a wheelchair who immediately grabbed my attention. She was sleeping in the wheelchair and had pipes coming out of her nose and mouth. She also had her family members around her and they looked unhappy and stressed.

That image of the little baby and the old woman made me notice something. Both of them had a common element in their lives. And what was that element? They were both helpless and depended on their family members for every little thing. Yet, their helplessness was so different. The helplessness of the baby aroused emotions of love, excitement, and hope in her family members. On the other hand, the helplessness of the old woman aroused the emotions of sadness, stress, and hopelessness in her family members. The helplessness of the baby was temporary. Within a few years, she will learn how to walk and run, and after that, she will spend a long life doing various exciting things to make her life good. But the helplessness of the old woman was perhaps permanent. She had no chance of standing up, walking, and running. To put it bluntly, she was on her deathbed.

Human life is a cycle that starts from helplessness and ends with helplessness. We have crossed the first kind of helplessness and one day, we will find ourselves in the second type. And when we will find ourselves in the second type of helplessness, we will surely feel that we are close to death and we will try to evaluate the life we have lived. This stage of life will give us a new perspective. So far, we thought that we had infinite time on the earth and we didn't bother much about questioning the way we lived. But on the deathbed, we will be able to look at the entire life we have lived and question ourselves if it was the best way to spend this earthly life. It might make us see the mistakes we have made and realise the way in which we could have lived better. The deathbed is a strange place. It gives us a lot of insights about life, but it doesn't offer any opportunity to put those insights into practice. By the time we learn things, it's too late.

There are some wonderful books which have been written on the basis of the experiences of people who were on their deathbeds. They felt a strong awareness of death, and this awareness taught them a lot about how to live a meaningful and joyful life, about what matters and what doesn't matter in life, and what are the mistakes we should avoid to enhance the quality of our life. These people imparted the knowledge they had gained while waiting for the last moment of human existence, but sadly, they didn't have enough time to use that knowledge in their own life to make it better. Reading such books can surely help us, but there is a limitation to the learning we can absorb from other people's experiences. After all, others' experiences are others' experiences, and nothing teaches us better than our own experiences.

You might have a question in your mind after reading the previous paragraph. Am I suggesting that we should wait for a crisis or catch a deadly disease and reach our own deathbed to learn things about living a better life? No, I am not suggesting that. We don't need to be close to our death to develop awareness of death. We don't need to put our life in danger to understand what death can teach us about life. We can develop awareness of death and get its benefits while we are healthy, strong, and energetic. We can do it today. Actually, it's more practical to develop awareness of death while we have a long and healthy life left with us because then we can use its knowledge to make our life more meaningful. But how can we do this? Let's take a learning tip from Japan.

Japan is a country of 6,852 islands, the world's deepest underwater post-box, the world's shortest poetry, the world's first novel, and Sumo wrestling. As if that's not enough, Japan is also the country with around five thousand earthquakes every year, most of which go unnoticed. But some of these earthquakes are immensely disastrous and calamitous. The Great Kanto Earthquake was the worst one in Japanese history. It killed over 100,000 people. In January 1995, another strong earthquake hit the city of Kobe and its surroundings. It killed 6,000 and injured 415,000 people. On March 11, 2011, the strongest ever recorded earthquake in Japan triggered a massive tsunami along the Pacific Coast of north-eastern Japan. It led to the death of nearly 20,000 people and caused a nuclear accident at a power plant in Fukushima Prefecture.

So, how do the Japanese people deal with these earthquakes? They have a very systematic approach towards staying prepared and reducing the number of casualties. One of the things they do is to organise earthquake drills regularly in primary schools. Schoolchildren are taught to seek protection and stay safe if they are hit by an earthquake. They are trained to get under their desks and hold onto their table legs until the earthquake is over. They are taught to go straight to the centre of an open space if they are playing outside which will save them from being killed by the falling debris.

In other words, these children are taught to imagine being in an earthquake so that they can handle an actual earthquake better whenever it comes. We will be applying the same principle for developing the awareness of death. We will be using our imagination and other tools to understand how it feels to be near death and then we will be using this experience to enhance our awareness and understanding of this helpful friend.

We will be using many exercises which people have been practising for thousands of years to develop the required awareness. We can learn from them and practice most of these exercises at the comfort of our home with a little mental effort, without putting ourselves into any kind of danger or crisis. In the next part of the book, we will go into the zone where very few people dare to venture.

We have made up our mind to start this unique journey of ten thousand miles. It's time to take the first step.

Part 2

HOW TO DEVELOP
AWARENESS OF DEATH

*"It's all God's will: you can die in your sleep,
and God can spare you in battle."*
— Leo Tolstoy, *War and Peace*

Chapter 4

LET'S GO TO OUR OWN FUNERAL

"In every wisdom tradition, there is a teaching called 'dying unto death', as the New Testament calls it. This means experiencing the truth about dying while you are still alive. At this moment, your body could not be alive without death. Billions of cells have to perish to bring new ones to life. You could not think or feel or dream if your mind did not allow your old thoughts to die away and make room for the new."

— Deepak Chopra, *The Deeper Wound: Recovering the Soul from Fear and Suffering*

If you ever go to Bangkok, you might want to visit Kid Mai Death Awareness Café. It's an exceptional café which offers a tempting combination of coffee and coffin.

When you enter the café, you will have to walk along a dark alley with signs which will have questions like 'Are you tired today?' and 'What's the purpose of your life?' In the middle of the café, you will find a traditional full-sized Thai coffin. You can choose to get into the coffin and lie down there for a few minutes. There are a few benefits of doing this. First, you will get a discount on the beverage you consume at the café. Second, as the Thai belief says, you will get rid of some of your bad karma when you come out of the coffin.

But it's the third benefit that matters the most. Spending some time in a coffin is not an easy and pleasant thing to do. It may fill you with uncomfortable emotions because it will arouse the fear which you have kept hidden in your subconscious. Inside the coffin, you will be able to imagine your death in its eerie darkness. When the lid of the coffin is closed, you might feel that the outer world where you have lived for so many years has vanished like a long dream. You can probably hear what others are saying outside the coffin, but there is no way you can speak to them. That life is over. You might feel a wave of fear inside for leaving that world or you might feel the peace and relaxation which this ultimate sleep might bring. Or you can even feel something which you have never expected before.

Irrespective of what you feel and experience, the minutes you spend there can be immensely useful. They can prepare us for an inevitable event of life which is waiting for each of us. Sooner or later, we all will have to enter our coffins without any prospect of coming out of them. Isn't it better to have a little imaginary experience of it before we face the real one?

You must have figured out by now that the place is not called Death Awareness Café without a reason. The whole café has been designed in a way that we can suspend our denial of death for a while and develop some awareness of death. According to the Buddha, when we understand that we are going to die, we will have a better understanding of what matters in life and we will also develop more compassion and selflessness for others. Remember that a cup of hot coffee can keep us awake for a few hours but a small experience in a coffin can keep us awake the whole life.

Taking a flight to Bangkok and visiting that café could be a good way to develop awareness of death. But most of us won't have the time and money to do that. So, there is a better way to get the same effect in our bedroom with a little free time and some imagination. We will need an uninterrupted hour to do this experiment. You can conduct it in your bedroom or some private place where you can spend some time in solitude. You can also switch off your cell phone so that there's no distraction.

Now let's begin with practising your own funeral. Lie down in a bed or on the floor and imagine that you are dead. Make this image vivid and detailed. You can take a few deep breaths so that your mind becomes calm. A calm mind is the best source of good mental images. Take a good look at your body. It's lying without making any movement. You cannot even raise your finger or move your eyelids because you are not alive anymore. Your lifeless body is lying in a coffin or on a funeral pyre. Feel the hardness of the surface of the coffin or the touch of the wooden blocks. It's a cremation ground, and you are here to say a final goodbye to people.

Let's give the picture some time to manifest on your mental screen. Those of us who haven't tried visualisation before might find it tough to imagine this scenario but we need to have patience and keep trying. Very soon the images will start coming to your mental screen. It's okay if those images are not very clear. You can further add to your visualisation by imagining your surroundings. You can imagine your family members, friends, and other acquaintances standing around you, looking at the dead body.

This exercise is going to be tough and uncomfortable because you are not visualising something pleasant. You are imagining probably the most tragic event of your life. You are confronting your biggest fear. After years of ignoring this ultimate reality of life, you are finally trying to see it face to face.

Now let's ask a few questions to ourselves. How would it feel to be incapable of using any word to communicate our feelings? How would it feel to see the sad and gloomy faces of our loved ones? How would it feel to lose everything— our family, money, possessions, career, clothes, body, dreams and one hundred other things—forever and accept the reality that we are never going to get them again? How would it feel to be dead?

This experiment is hard. I would like to share my own experiences which might be helpful to the readers. When I had done this experiment for the first time during my college days, I didn't feel anything for the first fifteen minutes. But after that, the imagination started feeling real to me. It felt so real that I went through an explosion of emotions inside me which led to an unbreakable stream of tears through my eyes. I wept and wept. For the first time, I realised how it might feel to lose everybody and everything. I felt the pain, the helplessness, and the sadness. But after that, I started experiencing immense peace in my heart and an unsurpassable clarity in my mind. I could clearly see how I had been living my life so far and how I had chosen the wrong priorities. It's only at the end of a movie when we realise the faults in the storyline. I had confronted the biggest fear of mankind, and the results were not scary at all. On the contrary, they were pleasant and emotionally fulfilling.

Your experiences might be similar or different from mine but there is one thing for sure—they will be insightful. It's better to keep at least one hour free for this experiment when we are doing it for the first time. This experiment might lead to unexpected feelings and emotions which you would like to go through intensely without any interruption. You can also write down your experiences in a journal. After all, this will be your first experience with your death even though it's imaginary. It's also useful to keep a record of what you felt and experienced.

After doing this experiment, you can congratulate yourself for taking this bold step. You have done something really concrete to develop awareness of death, and this experience is going to play an important role in shaping your life afterwards. Once you have done this experiment, sit for a while and think about your life. Ask yourself if you are really living the life you should be living. Do you know what really matters in your life? And if you don't know, shouldn't you try to find it out? If you really have to die one day, how should you make the best use of your limited time on the earth?

You can also choose to repeat this experiment again and again to make the awareness of death stronger in your mind. You can choose to practice it once a week or once a month, that's up to you.

Developing the awareness of death will make us a little uncomfortable initially, but it will give long term benefits throughout our life. We will discuss the benefits in another section of the book, but before that, we should find out more ways to make this awareness stronger and stronger so that it breaks the wall of denial we have built in our mind.

After seeing the benefits of this exercise, it's time to step out of our house to visit a unique kind of university on the coming weekend. No entrance test is needed to get admission there. It doesn't use books, teachers, or classrooms but can impart the most profound lessons of life.

Chapter 5

LET'S MAKE A TRIP TO THE GREATEST UNIVERSITY IN THE WORLD

"I found myself thinking about President
William McKinley, the third American
president to be assassinated. He lived for
several days after he was shot, and towards
the end, his wife started crying and screaming,
'I want to go too! I want to go too!' And with
his last measure of strength, McKinley turned
to her and spoke his last words: 'We are all
going.'"
— John Green, *Looking for Alaska*

When I had visited Nigambodh Ghat, one of the biggest and oldest cremation grounds of India, years back, I had noticed a wonderful line written by a famous Hindi poet, Jayashankar Prasad, on the signboard of one of its gates. It said: "Death is the biggest silent teacher in the world. There is no need to fear it."

And there could be no better place to meet this silent teacher than a cremation ground. When we see dozens of tombs in a graveyard or watch many dead bodies turning into ashes, we realise there is a lot we can learn from here if we stay alert to our thoughts.

Cremation grounds are a part of the world, but so different from the world. The world we see around us is full of life, laughter, and hopes for a great future. It makes us feel that life will just go on and on without interruption. It promises that it will offer us great opportunities to fulfil many, if not all, dreams we have for tomorrow. But cremation grounds offer the other side of the picture which is not any less real. People from every age group, community, economic class, colour, caste, and creed come here, lying in coffins or bamboo cots. Most of them had been nourishing dreams like us till one day back. They had been planning for a bigger house, a bigger car, a better salary, a nice vacation, or more recognition in the society just like we are doing right now. But then their lives came to a full stop. Their dreams and plans and grudges vanished like dewdrops in the late morning.

It's a great truth we can learn at this unique and great university and it can change our perspective towards life. All we need to do is spend some time wisely at this place which brings us face to face with the reality we choose to ignore in the outer world. But we need to visit this place with a student's mindset to learn this truth. That's what we are discussing here.

Many times we go to cremation grounds to see off the loved ones who have just passed away. It can certainly bring some awareness of death in us but on those occasions, the places are crowded and we have to behave in a formal way, and that's why we don't get enough time and solitude to contemplate and meditate over the biggest reality of life. So, it's a great idea to visit those cremation grounds when we have plenty of time and nobody to accompany us so that we can just sit there and let the idea of death sink in our mind and heart. Maybe we can plan a weekend to spend there when we are free enough to give a couple of hours without any interruption. This idea might seem crazy and scary. Why would somebody want to waste a nice holiday in a place which is full of sadness and melancholy? But this idea has been followed by millions of people for thousands of years in many spiritual traditions who wanted to learn how to live by understanding how life ends. And they were immensely benefitted by it.

You might ask, "What shall I do there?" The answer is nothing much. The less you do the better results you will get. Let's just sit there and do nothing. Let's watch the tombs and think about those people who must be lying inside there. Let's have a look at the corpses which are slowly burning on the funeral pyres. When you see flames coming out of a lifeless human body, just observe how the one million desires of a man turn into nothingness in a minute. When you see a body being pushed into a grave, try to feel how the dreams to fly high finally get a permanent residence six feet under the earth. When you see the family members leaving the place after disposing the corpse, understand that nobody and nothing is going to assist us when we stop breathing. The lifelong incessant struggle to build good relationships and seek comfort in others' company finally leads to ultimate loneliness in the end. There is an old saying about the human body: it comes from the earth, and it goes back to the earth. Let's realise that sooner or later we all are going to meet the same fate. We are not going to live forever. The flames that were burning another body will soon engulf ours. The grave which swallowed a dead person just now will be waiting for us with its open jaws. Let's remember that we will go to them naked, we won't carry any of our possessions with us, and we will step into the next journey alone.

These thoughts seem clichéd, but they are as true and eternal as the sun and the moon. These thoughts don't make an effect on our lives because we just hear them and read them, but in reality, we don't understand them and we don't feel them. We think these things happen only to others and we are safe from them. Cremation grounds are the places where we can understand them, we can feel them, and we can make them a part of our living reality. Therefore, I call crematoriums the greatest universities as they can teach us things that can alter our way of thinking and transform our lives for the better.

Most probably, just one visit to the place may not have a strong and long-lasting effect. It may not create the desired awareness of death which will make a difference in your life. That's why it is suggested that you visit the place again and again. Actually, you can make it a part of your regular life to spend some time there once in a while. Maybe you can make a promise to yourself that you will visit the place once a month or once a year. Just like a hammer can push a nail deep into a hard surface by hitting it again and again, you should also let the awareness of death make a deep impression on your mind by visiting that place again and again. Therefore, frequent visits to cremation grounds will give you more opportunities to contemplate over death and learn things about life you cannot learn anywhere else.

We all will visit this place at the end of our life, but by then, it will be too late and it won't be able to teach us anything. So, we should approach this place for its great teachings while we are conscious, healthy, and inquisitive. We should use this place which is a goldmine of insights to add a deep perspective to our lives. Thus, we should make sure that we put the visits to cremation grounds in our things-to-do list and go there with the learner's mindset at least once a year.

The quest to arouse awareness of death doesn't end here. No university in the world can impart anything if we don't spend some time in self-study. After learning the basics from the cremation grounds, we can make use of the spare minutes we find here and there every day to improve our awareness. And we don't even need to get off the couch to do that.

Chapter 6

LET'S TURN THOSE SPARE MINUTES INTO SEEDS OF ENLIGHTENMENT

*"During meditation, practice dying while
still alive. That is, leave your body, discard
it, and float above the world. This will help
you disconnect yourself from feeling that your
physical shell is who you are. The more you are
the observer rather than the object of what you
see, the easier it will be to remove your fear
of dying. Do this for just a few minutes daily.
Remember that you are not this body—you are
a piece of the infinite Tao, never changing and
never dying."*
— Wayne Dyer, *Change Your Thoughts,
Change Your Life*

The Secret Life of Walter Mitty is an interesting movie. Its main character, Walter Mitty, is just like most of us. He lives a very boring and ordinary life that doesn't offer the kind of excitement or adventure he seeks earnestly. So, he finds out an easy solution to this problem: whenever he gets some free time, he starts daydreaming about different adventures in his life. In his dreams, he photographs leopards in Afghanistan, travels on ships across oceans filled with sharks, jumps from a helicopter, saves his office crush's life, and does many things he couldn't do in his real and boring life. His daydreaming is his escape from the mundane life he has to live.

For Indians, the old Hindi TV serial *Mungerilal Ke Haseen Sapne* could be the best reference. In this serial, in each episode, the protagonist, Mungerilal, has a new dream in which he does things that are impossible to do in real life. In one episode, he becomes a brave army officer who fights on the border; in another episode, he becomes the boss of his office and scolds his real-life boss; and in another episode, he dates his office crush. He keeps enjoying these dreams till they are broken by the slap of reality.

Walter Mitty and Mungerilal may make us laugh at their fantasies, but aren't we doing the same thing in our lives, too? Whenever we get some spare time, we start dreaming about becoming a famous person, driving swanky cars, defeating others in political discussions with our sharp logic, looking hot and sexy, becoming the most popular chap in our community, winning awards, holidaying in exotic islands, and doing one million other things which give us quick pleasure. We keep looking for a sweet and fake escape from the realities of life. They give us instant pleasure and seem to cost nothing.

But instead of escaping into our fantasies, what if we take a different approach? What if we change our attitude and start facing the reality in our spare moments? What if we start utilising those spare minutes in developing the awareness of death? Many of us won't like this idea. A fake and pleasant escape is easier to handle than a genuine and unpleasant confrontation with reality, especially if that reality involves something scary and depressing like death. But then, a fake escape cannot help us live deeply and enjoy the contentment and meaningfulness we deserve. If we want to collect precious pearls, we need to develop the courage to dive deep into an ocean. Enjoying a bottle of beer on the beach won't help us get those pearls.

So, from now on, let's start doing something new. Whenever we get a spare minute, let's think about our death. Let's remind ourselves that this life is going to be over soon. Let's make a quick mental picture of our funeral pyre or grave. Let this image sink deep into our consciousness so that we never forget it in the fast pace and distractions of life. If possible, try to do it many times a day. You can do it while waiting for your cab, bus, or train and while standing in the grocery line or at a red traffic light. You can do it while waiting for your computer to start and while waiting for the tea to boil on the stove. You can also do it once before you go to sleep. You should do it so often that the awareness of death becomes a burning reality in your thoughts and feelings. I call these minutes 'one-minute awareness pills' which we should consume many times a day.

So far, we had been wasting those leisure moments in finding superficial imaginary pleasures which made us feel good but didn't add anything to the quality of our life. But now, we are investing those moments in developing the awareness of death which will open the doors to a more meaningful, joyful, and beautiful life. We can be sure that every minute we spend strengthening awareness of death will work as a seed for a better life. And with time, those seeds will grow into the giant trees of awareness which will become the launch pad for a life full of purpose and intensity.

While gulping down these seeds, we can give another push to the desired awareness by preparing a small document. Most of us write this document so that others can refer to it. But this time, we will write this document so that we can refer to it. And if prepared sincerely, it can work as the best lighthouse in the voyage of life.

Chapter 7

Let's Write Today What We are Supposed to Write in the End

*"Death is like a mirror in which the true
meaning of life is reflected."*
— Sogyal Rinpoche, *The Tibetan Book of
Living and Dying*

$\mathcal{L}$et me tell you the story of Croesus. He was the last king of Lydia and was so affluent that till today, Romans use the expression 'as rich as Croesus' for somebody who is extraordinarily wealthy. One day, a philosopher named Solon came to meet the king. He was one of the Seven Sages of Greece and had also laid down the laws of the Athenian democracy.

It was a meeting between the richest and the wisest. The richest man showed his immense wealth and power to the wisest man, but the wisest man didn't look even a bit impressed. This kind of response shook Croesus a bit because many ambitious people acquire great riches to impress others, and if somebody is not impressed with their wealth, it hurts their self-confidence. Then Croesus got an idea. He asked Solon to tell the name of the happiest man he had come across in his life. Croesus was sure that Solon would try to flatter him by taking his name since he had immense wealth, and wealth is generally considered to be a synonym of happiness. Solon took the name of a gentleman called Tellus the Athenian. He explained his choice by saying that Tellus was neither rich nor poor, his children were noble, and he died with dignity while fighting for his country.

Not pleased with Solon's answer, Croesus asked him the name of the second happiest man. Solon gave the name of another man called Agalus and said that he was so happy living on his farm that he never left it, and he died surrounded by his happy family. Croesus's displeasure increased and he asked Solon the names of other happiest people. Again, Solon named two people who were not very rich or powerful but lived a happy and satisfied life.

Now Croesus couldn't control his impatience and he asked Solon why he couldn't name Croesus as the happiest person after seeing his unfathomable wealth and power. Then Solon replied that people didn't know what the future would bring tomorrow, and we could call a person happy only after seeing his last day on the earth. He couldn't call Croesus the happiest person on the earth because he had seen many powerful people die an unfortunate death and it would be too early to give him this title before seeing his entire life.

Croesus was naturally not happy with the answer, but he didn't discuss the matter any further and forgot about Solon after a few days. A few years later, Croesus lost his son who had gone hunting and died of a fatal wound. Very soon, Cyrus the Great, the powerful Persian king, attacked and captured Croesus at his palace. They built a great pyre and put the once-mighty king on it to burn him to death. It was at that moment that Croesus remembered Solon's words and called his name with a sad voice. Cyrus was surprised to hear Solon's name and asked Croesus the reason behind calling his name. Then Croesus told him what Solon had said about judging the happiness of a man and said that his wise words were worth more than all the riches and glory of the world. Cyrus was so touched by Solon's words that he pardoned Croesus and made him his friend.

This wonderful story makes an important point that we cannot judge our happiness until we have seen our last day on earth. Our last day makes us understand our life much better because only then we can see our life in its totality. Since we are not going to wait till that day comes, we will be doing a small exercise today to get the similar insights. Let's imagine that your life will be over tonight. The doctors have given their final word and it's time to leave. Now you are supposed to write that final piece of paper that will tell people how you are going to distribute your property and what should be done with your belongings after your departure. In short, you are going to write your will.

So, I suggest that you should take an hour or two off from the daily commitments to write your imaginary will. But a question that arises is that what shall I write there? You can write how your property and belongings should be distributed. You can write how your money should be used after you are gone. But that's not enough. You can add a piece about what you feel about the life you have lived so far and some advice that you would like to give to the people who are left behind. You can also write about the good decisions you took and the bad decisions you have made. Most importantly, you can write about the level of happiness you had experienced in your life. Can you say that you have lived a happy life? If your answer is yes, then what are the things which made you happy? If your answer is no, then what are the things which made you unhappy? You can also add a paragraph on how you would prefer to live your life if given another chance to live for twenty more years. What are the changes you will make and what are the mistakes you won't repeat to live happier?

It's a very useful exercise which not only develops the awareness of death but also makes us analyse the way we are living. When we write our imaginary will, we feel the intensity of the last day which will come eventually. It's also a good idea to refer to that imaginary will from time to time and edit things as our perspective develops. By doing that, we will keep enforcing that idea in our head that this physical life is not everlasting and we should always expect the end of this journey one day. This imaginary will can enforce the awareness of death in our mind so deep that it will influence our way of living and the choices we make for our whole life. This imaginary will can also work as a source of inspiration for the kind of life we strive to live. There is no point in waiting for the last day of our life to write our will. Let's do it as soon as possible.

So far, we have used the concept of our own death to develop the awareness. Now it's time to seek help from others. Every day they are leaving a great message for us and we shouldn't miss it.

Chapter 8

WHEN WE LOSE A LOVED ONE, WE SHOULDN'T LOSE THE LESSON

"Many have died; you also will die. The drum
of death is being beaten. The world has fallen
in love with a dream. Only sayings of the wise
will remain."
— Kabir, *The Bijak of Kabir*

A friend of mine, let's call him Aman, had told me his love story that I can never forget. He had fallen in love with a girl who used to study in his college ten years back. During college days, they were nothing more than acquaintances whose conversations never went beyond "How are the classes going?" The girl had a very impressive and charming personality which Aman always noticed and admired. But there was nothing beyond that.

Their lives took different routes after the college days and they lost touch with each other. But as luck would have it, they met again later, through a social media site. By then, Aman was enjoying his singlehood and the girl had married somebody but was separated. She also had a child from her previous marriage. After they reconnected, the girl sensed the admiration Aman had for her, and very soon the admiration turned into love which was fairly reciprocated by the girl.

They lived thousands of kilometres apart, but their love grew through the long phone conversations they used to have. Beneath the charming and smart personality, the girl hid her emotional wounds of the failed relationship and a strong feeling of loneliness. She told Aman that her uncle had affectionately told her that she should get married because life is long and it could be very lonely if she stayed single. Aman understood her pain and this empathy enhanced his love. They planned to meet soon and spend some lovely time with each other.

Then one morning, Aman got a message from her in which she said she was not sure if she would be able to get married to him or not. She said only destiny would decide what would happen to their relationship. Aman couldn't understand the reason behind this sudden change in her behaviour. He tried calling and messaged her again and again but all of them remained unanswered. Aman respected her decision and privacy and didn't try to bother her again. But once in a while, he always sent a polite message asking about her life.

Then one day, which was the last day of a year, he got a phone call from a common friend. The friend told him that the girl had passed away a few days back, and she was cremated by her family members. Aman got the shock of his life. He felt as if he had been pushed off a cliff, and there was an unending abyss he was falling into. In the next few weeks, Aman talked to his old college friends and the picture became clearer to him. When their love was at its peak, the girl found out that she was suffering from cancer and didn't know whether she would survive or not. It was in those days that she had sent that message to him as she didn't want him to be a part of her sufferings. She wanted to keep it to herself and didn't want to increase his pain by saying a final goodbye to him. The selflessness of her love made Aman's love for her grow stronger and stronger. He also realised how transient life could be and it should never be taken for granted. The death of his loved one left a deep impression on him which is still there without losing its intensity.

Aman's story may look unique but its essence is very common. We all have lost our loved ones, and many times, we didn't get a chance to say goodbye to them. This is the eternal truth of life. We will lose all of our loved ones one by one or our loved ones will lose us one day. No force in the world can change this reality. And what do we do when we lose our loved ones? After the initial shock and sadness, slowly we try to forget the pain it caused us and then we move on with our lives. We think we won't be able to live further if we dwell on the pain and memories. It's true that we shouldn't dwell on the pain but it's also true that we shouldn't forget an important lesson here. Every loved one who leaves the world gives us the lesson that sooner or later, we all have to leave this earthly life. One by one, death will come to all of us. And it's not that we don't know this fact, it's just that we don't feel the emotional intensity of this fact. The death of a loved one gives us that emotional intensity because of the feelings and intimacy we have for that person.

This exercise requires us to remember all those people we have lost and think about the lesson they have indirectly given to us. In this chaos of modern life, let's keep that flame of remembrance alive so that we don't forget the day when we will be gone forever.

So, whenever you get some free time, think about somebody you loved who has left this world. Think about the joyful moments you spent with that person. Let their voice echo in your ears and how you felt when you touched them. Let the emotions of love and nostalgia and pain come up and spread over your heart. Then think about their departure and let it make you understand that none of us is here forever. One day, we also will vanish from the earth, and our loved ones will miss us. Let's make sure that we remember this precious lesson.

We all are standing in a queue. The departure of a loved one reminds us that our turn will come soon. While we mourn for the ones who have left us, we should also remember the lesson they have left for us.

In this journey, strangers can be as helpful as our loved ones. If we are alert enough, we can get their assistance from all over the world. It's time to allow them to offer a helping hand.

Chapter 9

IF WE WANT THE MESSAGE, EVERYBODY CAN BE A MESSENGER

"It is crucial to be mindful of death—to contemplate that you will not remain long in this life. If you are not aware of death, you will fail to take advantage of this special human life that you have already attained. It is meaningful since, based on it, important effects can be accomplished."

— Dalai Lama, *Advice on Dying: And Living a Better Life*

$\mathcal{L}$et me ask you a question: what is the safest place in the world? Do you think it is your home? According to a study published in the Journal of General and Family Medicine in March 2017, every year, around 19,000 people die by drowning in their bathtubs in Japan alone. If you think your beds are safe, then consider this: as per Centers for Disease Control and Prevention, 10,386 people died due to falling from bed in the USA from 1999 to 2014. These are not small numbers.

You might think then that open grounds are safe? But in two states of India, Bihar and Uttar Pradesh, more than 100 people were killed by lightning in a single day in 2020. A few years back, an entire football team of eleven in Eastern Kasai, a province of the Democratic Republic of the Congo, were struck by lightning while playing in an open playground. Also, according to National Geographic, annually about 2,000 people are killed worldwide by lightning.

Let's change the track a little bit. We all have heard the saying that laughter is the best medicine but laughter can kill too. In 1556, the influential Italian author and libertine, Pietro Aretino, died of suffocation from laughing too much at a joke during a meal in Venice. Well, even too much appreciation can kill somebody. In 620 BC, an Athenian lawmaker was surrounded by admirers at the theatre in Aegina. They showered so many cloaks and hats on him to show their appreciation that he was smothered to death. Surprisingly, people can get killed even if they are being guarded by extremely powerful armies and the top security personnel in the world. Abraham Lincoln, John F. Kennedy, Indira Gandhi, James Garfield, Yitzhak Rabin, and Julius Caesar are some of the prominent examples in this category.

The moral of these stories is that there is nothing called as absolute safety from death. There is no place in the world secure enough to guarantee full protection from being dead. We can find plenty examples of people dying of random causes all over the world on news channels and newspapers. These people can be rich or poor, powerful or powerless, healthy or diseased, white or black, male or female, and young or old. It hardly matters as death spares no one. If it chooses to pick up somebody, the deal is done.

The fact is that out of all the people who die, most of them don't expect their end to come so soon. Like us, they were thinking that they had decades of life left with them and would have never guessed that their end would soon be approaching. They had plans, they had dreams, they had ambitions, they had aspirations, and they had the faith that they would live enough to execute them. Thus, these people are messengers to the rest of us who are still here. They are indirectly telling us that we shouldn't ignore the possibility of death like most of them did.

But they are not the only ones who are giving this message. If we are really keen on developing awareness of death, everybody and everything can be of immense help. We can look at dead insects and understand how life ends for everybody. We can pick up dry leaves and see that even they are not exempt from this ultimate reality. We can go to a restaurant and have a look at the non-vegetarian dishes. The animals and birds used in making those dishes were alive just some time ago. Even the vegetarian elements had life in them till a few hours or days back. We can also go to historical sites and think about those people who had built them hundreds of years ago. They were alive and active like us and had dreamt beautiful scenarios and planned wonderful things about their life. They too must have enjoyed their families, friends, careers, hobbies, and food like we are doing now. But where are they now? Not only that, even non-animate objects can remind us of the impermanence of life. We can look at a broken cup, think about an old and useless car that has been sold to scrap dealers, and observe a torn cloth. Millions of such things were 'alive' in their own way some time back. But now they are no more. Even their lives are not permanent. The fact of the matter is that nothing lasts forever.

Everyday life keeps reminding us through dozens of events and things that it's not going to stay forever. It will come to an end, probably sooner than we think. We shouldn't try to turn a blind eye to this fact; we shouldn't try to ignore this reality. We must embrace it. We must make it a guideline for living our life. We must use it to keep ourselves alert to our true priorities. So, from now on, whenever we see or read any news about death, let's not skip it. Let's stay with the news for a minute or two. Whenever we see something dead or broken, let's think about the impermanence of life. Let's use every opportunity to strengthen our awareness.

If we want to work a bit harder, we can also maintain a folder containing news clips on deaths. Going through that collection once in a while will refresh our awareness of death. It will make us remember what we keep forgetting from time to time. It will remind us that we also have limited time on the planet, just like the ones who became a subject of those news clips.

After going this far on our journey, you might feel that it could be tiresome to travel alone on this path. In the next chapter, we will discuss how one can find some co-travellers to make this journey more fruitful.

Chapter 10

THE JOURNEY WILL BE BETTER IF
WE FIND A CO-TRAVELLER

"We are all travelers in the wilderness of
the world, and the best we can find
in our travels is an honest friend."
— Robert Louis Stevenson

There was a touchy and honest line written outside a crematorium I can never forget: 'Thanks for coming with us so far. From here on, we will travel alone.' It's true that once we leave this earthly life, none of our friends and family members will be with us on the aftermath journey. We will have to travel alone. But before that moment comes, we can make our journey easier and more meaningful by finding somebody who thinks like us.

It won't be easy to find such people. We live in a society that has turned death into a source of entertainment by making it a part of crime literature and movies. We enjoy watching others dying in crime shows, documentaries, and live telecast of wars on news channels. But when it comes to our own death or the death of our close ones, our lips become sealed. We deny this matter as if it doesn't exist at all.

Thankfully, there are some people who think otherwise. They accept the impermanence of human life and face this truth with pure honesty. They would love to discuss this subject if they find somebody who is equally interested in this matter.

But how can we find such people? Maybe you can randomly try to discuss this subject with friends and acquaintances. You can be sure that most of them will either ignore the subject by becoming silent or divert the conversation to some other direction. But once in a while, you will find somebody who will listen to you with an attentive face and talk about their own experiences and thoughts with equal sincerity. You can also try to find courses and workshops available on the subject of death. I had attended one wonderful course organised by Tushita Meditation Centre in Dharamsala, India, which was called 'Peaceful Living, Peaceful Dying'. In this course, Buddhist monks taught us how to prepare ourselves and our loved ones for a peaceful death. You can find like-minded people in such courses.

If you cannot find such people, you can always rely on books. Many insightful books have been written by people who have dealt with dying people or had a direct experience with death. You can create your own bookshelf which will have such books related to this subject. You can take refuge in these books and absorb the thoughts of their authors to strengthen your awareness. I call these books 'the mental monastery'. Despite living in a modern city and being a part of the urban lifestyle, we can create a monastery-like atmosphere in our mind with the help of this bookshelf which will keep us focussed towards developing awareness of death. I have given a list of such books at the end of this book in 'Recommended Readings'. They can be helpful to the seekers.

And when we find such people and books, we must treasure them. They are going to be our co-travellers on the path to awareness of death. They are going to be our rare assets in life. We will find ourselves having an honest discussion with these people on this subject many times which will benefit both sides.

This is the end of Part Two. So far, we have discussed various methods to develop an awareness of death. If we practice even one of them, we will notice our attitude towards life going through a radical change. With this changed attitude, we will start seeing some benefits which have been described in the next few chapters.

Part 3

THE BENEFITS OF THE AWARENESS OF DEATH

"The moment you accept what troubles you've been given, the door will open."
— Jalaluddin Rumi

Chapter 11

FINDING OUT WHAT WE TRULY WANT

*"Depend upon it, sir, when a man knows he is
to be hanged in a fortnight, it concentrates his
mind wonderfully."*
— Samuel Johnson, *The Life of Samuel
Johnson LL.D. Vol. 3*

On June 12, 2005, the graduating students of one of the
finest universities in the world had gathered to listen to a
gentleman who was not even a graduate. That gentleman
shared three stories about how he went from being the
undesired biological son of an unwed young woman to
becoming the founder of several top companies which
brought a revolution in the field of personal computers and
the art of animation film-making.

His last story was about how he had used the concept of
death to find out what he wanted to do in life and develop
the courage to do it despite all odds. For thirty-three years,
every day he asked himself if he would be doing the things
he was doing if it was the last day of his life. It made him
question what he was doing and if the answer was 'no'
for many days, he understood that he needed to change
something in his life.

You might have guessed the name of the gentleman by
now. This man was none other than Steve Jobs. And we

can put ourselves in his shoes and ask the same question to ourselves again and again. Actually, we don't even need to ask this question every day if we have worked a bit to develop an awareness of death as described in the previous chapters. Asking it even once will direct our mind to find out what really matters in our life. But let's look further at how this approach can improve our overall quality of life.

When somebody is too rich, he loves splurging his money on things that don't matter. But when somebody has less money, he will try to spend it on the most essential things first. The same logic applies to the amount of time we think we have in life. If we think we have got decades to live, we will find ourselves spending our time on trivial pursuits. But if we think we have less time on the earth, we will try to find out what's really important to us so that we can spend the rest of our life doing that. Therefore, we can use our awareness of death to turn our mind into a magnet that attracts only the most important and essential things.

Keeping our imminent death in mind, we can ask ourselves if we would like to slog day and night so that we can have a better salary, if we really need to watch everything that TV and the internet offer, and if we really need to take part in long gossip sessions to find out what's going on in other people's lives. And sure enough, if we have an acute awareness of death, we wouldn't want to participate in such activities and instead do things that give true meaning and fulfilment to our life. This is because when we become aware of our death, every hour of our life starts to matter, just like for a person travelling in a desert, every drop of water is significant. This awareness turns us into a detective whose goal is to figure out what's truly essential, what's really important.

I have asked many people if they know what they truly want in their life. Most of them become quiet for a few minutes and say with a little embarrassment that they don't know what they actually want. They are living their lives unconsciously and have never thought that there could be another way to live. They don't realise that they could have original and unique desires which come from their inner self rather than society's expectations, fashion trends, and advertisements. They just go by the laundry list of things that were provided by their family, society, and elders. They never bothered to prepare their own list. This attitude is similar to sitting in a car and not knowing where we want to go. We watch where all other people are going and then we move our car in that direction. Another example that encapsulates this is like going to a tailor and not giving him the size of our shirt and instead asking him to make a shirt according to the most popular size in the market. In both of these examples, we end up living a standardised version of life and not a version of life that is meant for us.

If we could ask ourselves the question Steve Jobs asked himself every day, we too would realise what we truly want from life and what we really want to do while we are here. These answers may vary from person to person, but each answer would be genuine and full of inner conviction. There are also many ways to approach this idea. We can make a list of ten or twenty or fifty things we want to do before we die. We can ask ourselves what we would want to do if we had got only one year or one month or one day to live. We can visualise ourselves on funeral pyres and analyse the life we have lived so far. Then we can remember the things we regret doing and the things we regret not doing. We can think about the things which gave us maximum happiness and satisfaction. These things will surely guide us towards finding out things that truly matter in our lives. We must always remember that this life will be over too soon. It's way better to think about our death now and find out the things we want to do than to lie in our deathbed later on and regret doing things we didn't want to do. This awareness will teach us that direction is the most important part of a journey. It's more important than speed. But we focus too much on speed and feel proud about achieving things faster than others. That's why our society promotes and appreciates young achievers. Due to this, we end up giving less attention to finding out the right direction of our life. The truth is that we need to go deep into our mind and figure out our right destination before taking the next step in life. Maybe then we would be able to appreciate the 'right achievers' as it's wiser to achieve the right things a little late than to achieve the wrong things a little early.

There is an old and popular saying I love pondering over and which captures this emotion: 'I was so busy climbing the ladder of success that it was only at the top I realised that the ladder was leaning against the wrong wall'. Therefore we need to find out the right wall before stepping on the first rung of the ladder. And if we waste our entire life climbing the wrong wall and realise our mistake only at the end of our life, then there is nothing we will be able to do about it as by then, it will be too late.

The awareness of death also helps solve another problem that is common among old people. After crossing the age of sixty, many people realise that they have spent their lives majorly in two pursuits: family and career. But at this junction of time, none of these are available to keep them engaged. Their children have grown up, shifted to other places, and started their own families. They have also retired from their jobs and they don't know what to do with the time available after finishing their breakfast. This problem can be explained in a single word—aimlessness. They have plenty of spare time but don't know what to do with it. But if they have invested time in developing awareness of death, they will surely find out a third pursuit that will add meaning to their lives, and their spare time will be utilised in doing things that make them happier.

Clarity about priorities is the first benefit of awareness of death. It gives a true direction to our life and makes us passionately look for the things we truly want.

After figuring out what we want, it's time to discover a crucial element which is necessary to start the journey of pursuing it. That element is more important than talent, money, and a high level of energy.

Chapter 12

THE COURAGE TO LIVE THE LIFE WE WANT TO LIVE

"Life is not about living the safer option. Life is about living a life worth living."
— Robert Thier, *Storm and Silence*

$\mathcal{O}$nce upon a time, there lived an old man who was counting his last days on a hospital bed. Since he had lots of time to think, he decided to think about his own life. As he thought more about his life, he came to a sad realisation.

He realised he had wasted his seventy years doing the wrong things. He stayed stuck in a bad job which didn't fulfil him. He stayed married to a woman who was not happy with him. He lived in a place that didn't offer any opportunity for his growth. But why didn't he come out of these things when he had plenty of time? The answer was simple: he didn't have the courage. Since he couldn't tell himself that he was a coward, he kept telling himself that he will do something to come out of them the next month or the next year. But guess what? That next month or the next year never came. What came was a hospital bed which was going to be the last bed of his life.

This is not the story of one old man; this is the story of millions, or maybe even billions of men and women including us. Only when death comes really close, we realise that we didn't do many things we wanted to do because we didn't have enough courage to take the necessary steps. We justify our lack of courage by telling ourselves that we have a long life waiting for us, so we could postpone the decision as long as we wish.

But there is a way we can change this way of thinking. We can build the courage we require to go for the life we want to live by realising that we don't have unlimited time on earth. Let's go back to the speech of Steve Jobs we talked about in the last chapter. As we know, he asked himself every day if he would be doing what he was doing if it was the last day of his life. Apart from knowing what he truly wanted in his life, this question also made him realise that his life would be over soon and everything will be lost anyway. So, he came out of the trap of thinking that he had something to lose, and it made him lose all external expectations, all pride, and all fear of embarrassment. In other words, he lost the fear of failure for the things he wanted to do.

Now let's try ourselves what Steve Jobs did and try to imagine that today is the last day of our life. What shall we do then? Shall we postpone what we want to do to some other day or month? Shall we wait for a better time when we have more comfort and security to take the steps to achieve what we truly desire? No, we won't wait. We will realise that it's a now or never situation. We will start doing what we want to, without any delay.

Many times, we stay stuck in a bad relationship, place, or job because we fear that we will fall into something even worse if we leave them. No matter how bad our present situation is, it still gives us a sense of comfort and familiarity which we don't want to lose. But when we face the inevitability of death, we already put ourselves in the most uncomfortable position and transcend it. We confront the worst that can happen that makes us realise that our other fears are trivial compared to it. Let's understand it this way. Death is the biggest loss or setback that life can offer us. It takes away everything—our family, friends, money, possessions, dreams, reputation, social image, ambitions, our body, etc. When we accept that we have to die anyway and we have to lose everything for sure, our fear of losing other things becomes powerless. Then we start feeling the true courage required to do what we want.

I am reminded of a Japanese story which puts this point across perfectly. Centuries back, a Samurai felt badly offended after coming to know that his wife was having an affair with his servant. His honour was hurt, and he challenged his servant for a sword fight. The servant was hardly keen to participate in the fight because he stood no chance against the seasoned warrior who had been trained since his childhood and had fought in many battles. But he didn't have a choice. He had committed the crime of having an affair with the wife of a married man, and he couldn't refuse a fight with the man.

They met the next day at a chosen area where a huge crowd had gathered to watch the duel. Everybody knew the result of the fight, but they had come to watch the drama anyway. When the fight began, the bystanders realised that their expectation was not right. The servant was not trained in the fight, but he was fighting with his complete energy and passion. And though he didn't have proper training, his moves were deadly in a surprising way. The fight went on for an hour and by the end of it, the Samurai was lying on the ground with his bleeding chest and bruised body. More than the pain in his body, it was the shock in his eyes which made him worth a watch. He couldn't believe that he was defeated by a harmless and weak servant. When the servant was asked about the secret of his victory, he spoke in a mild voice, "When I came to fight, I was prepared for my death. When I became mentally prepared for my death, I knew I had nothing to lose. When I had nothing to lose, I was filled with unexpected courage. I became completely fearless and fought with my heart and soul, and that's why I am alive today."

In the face of death, none of our fears matter. They become insignificant. This is the alchemic magic of awareness of death that makes us fearless. There is another story that I would like to share here. Around 2000 years ago, Julius Caesar set out with his naval forces to conquer England. When he reached near the coast, he realised that his enemy's army was in a much greater number than his soldiers. This was a clear disadvantage to him. But that was not all. His soldiers were also tired after a long sea journey whereas his enemies were fresh and fully energetic. But Caesar had to take a decision. He knew very well that attacking a much bigger army sitting in a better position was almost like committing suicide. But he hadn't come so far only to go back. So, while his army was sleeping in the night, he decided to do something which nobody on the earth could have ever expected.

When his soldiers got up in the morning, they found that their boats had been burnt down. While they were recovering from the immense shock, Caesar called them and told them he had ordered the destruction of their boats. Now they couldn't make a retreat. They were left with only one option if they had to stay alive: they would have to win the war. Caesar's army fought with the kind of bravery and energy which his enemy couldn't fathom. They won the war, conquered England, and stayed alive to tell the tale.

We don't have to get into a swordfight with somebody or attack a country in order to come face to face with real death and awaken the courage which lies asleep in us. We can visualise our death and build some courage right now to do the things we want. Death ends our life. But the awareness of death gives us the courage to live our life the way we want to live. It seems ironic, but it's true.

While we need courage to do daring things in life, we also need something else which keeps our little anxieties and worries away. It is probably one of the most desired things in today's world which is full of fears and unpredictable events. Let's see how the awareness of death can help us find it.

Chapter 13

MENTAL PEACE AND LOSS OF FEAR

"What we believe becomes true for us. If you believe in hell, then you will probably go there for a while until you awaken to the truth and change your consciousness. I really believe that heaven and hell are states of mind, and we can experience both while here on earth. Fearing death interferes with living. It is not until we can be at peace with dying that we can really begin living."

— Louise L Hay, *LIFE!: Reflections on Your Journey*

When the black Mercedes Benz stopped in front of the modest ashram of the spiritual guru, nobody was surprised. It was common for people from the richest to the poorest sections of the society to come to the ashram and seek the guru's advice on the matters of life.

This time, the richest businessman of the city had come for a visit. He went inside the ashram and after greeting the guru, he spoke in his modest and sad voice, "Swami, I am a very rich man. This is the best thing about my life and this is also the worst thing about my life. Since I am rich, I enjoy a very luxurious life and a very powerful position in the city. Many people would like to exchange their lives with mine. But this money has also brought me so many anxieties, so many fears. I fear that I will lose my business. I fear that my son won't be able to handle it very well. That apart, I fear that my family will die. I fear that I will die. And unfortunately, this great amount of money has no cure for what's eating me from inside. I have tried everything. I have tried psychotherapy, chanting mantras, various forms of meditation, medicines, drugs, and prayers but nothing has worked. What should I do?"

The guru looked at him with compassionate eyes and said, "I won't ask you to try anything new. Just go to your home and face all your worries and fears. Accept that your worst fears might come true and you cannot do anything about it."

The businessman got the shock of his life. "I thought you would suggest a remedy," he spoke in a shivering voice, "but you ask me to face my fears. If I do that, I will die of heart attack."

The guru responded in a calming voice, "Trust me. You won't die."

After realising that the guru had nothing more to speak, the businessman got up and left. There was no sign of him for seven days. Then he showed up again at the ashram and this time, he seemed more calm and joyful. He met the guru and said, "I cannot believe what has happened. I had decided that I won't follow your advice as it seemed so scary to me. But then I thought you are a wise man and you won't suggest anything harmful. So, I closed my room and started thinking about all my worries and fears. Initially, I felt very upset and threatened. But after a while, I started feeling a sense of calm and mild joy. I realised that my worst fears seemed scary only if I tried to run away from them. I asked myself what would happen if all my fears and worries came true. And in that moment, I realised that in the worst case, I will have a peaceful death. I was unnecessarily taking myself and my worries too seriously. For the first time in many years, I had a nice sleep. I have slept like turtles the last seven days. Thank you! Thank you, swami."

Fear is a strange thing. It grows stronger when we run away from it and becomes weaker when we face it and accept it. Practising awareness of death is a great way to face and accept the most dreadful fear which is also the mother of all other fears. And when we develop an awareness of death, we realise that we are accepting the biggest fear of life. When we accept this gigantic fear, we stop resisting and avoiding it and we start feeling very peaceful.

Awareness of death also keeps our ego in check. It makes us realise how fragile our existence truly is. We start understanding that despite our money, power, and possessions, we are so helpless in front of the power of nature and that it can take away everything from us within a second. We recognise that our lives are going to be over very soon, and the world will easily go on without us. We begin to see that we are not as important as we want to believe and that we are not indispensable. This realisation brings in humility. Our ego starts losing its dominance, and its power and control also reduce. We find out that the desire to look bigger, richer, smarter, and more important than others is a big source of anxiety and it arises from the need of our ego to feed itself. And when that ego's need loses its strength, we start feeling peaceful and calm.

In a very popular story, a child asks a clay pot how it manages to stay so cool in summers. The clay pot replies, "I have come from the earth. I will go back to the earth.

Naturally, it's in my nature to stay cool like the earth." We all are like clay pots: our lives are transient, we too have come from the earth, and very soon, we will go back to the earth. This realisation lifts all burdens of life and brings mental peace.

When we think that our lives are infinitely long, our needs and desires also increase in the same proportion. Then we need too many things, we prepare too much, and we accumulate too many possessions. But when we realise that our life is short, we focus less on accumulating things and focus more on doing things that bring enjoyment right now. The relentless appetite for more and more things becomes weaker and we learn to enjoy whatever we have. We also start focussing more on being happy right now rather than making endless preparations for becoming happy in some future moment. This change in our habits and shift in our perspective enhances our tranquillity.

There is another story which I would like to share here. More than five centuries ago, the founder of the Sikh religion, Guru Nanak Dev, went to meet an arrogant rich man called Dhuni Chand at his palace. Dhuni Chand had put too many colourful flags at his house. He used to put one new flag for every one thousand rupees he earned and his aim was to earn one million rupees. He tried to impress Guru Nanak by organising a huge feast in his honour.

Guru Nanak appreciated the amount of money he had earned and made a request, "Please keep this needle with you. When we meet in the next life, please give this needle back to me. I would be very grateful for that."

Dhuni Chand was very happy for this honour from the great saint. He happily took the needle, but he couldn't sleep the whole night. He couldn't understand how he could carry the needle after his death. That was the day when he realised for the first time that he was not immortal and there was nothing he could carry with him after leaving this physical body. He had to leave everything behind—his palace, his money, his property, his oversized ego, as well as his flags.

The next day he went back to meet Guru Nanak and returned the needle. With a very calm and polite face, he said, "Thank you for teaching me the lesson. Now I realise that I cannot take anything with me when my time will be up." After this incident, Dhuni Chand was a new person. His ego had melted down and his mental anxiety for accumulating more and more was replaced by the mental peace generated by sharing his wealth with the needy. The awareness of death had done its magic in one more person's life.

On one hand, our changed mindset can fill us with mental peace to enjoy our life and on the other hand, it can also give us the mental strength to break the mountains. Let's see how it is possible.

Chapter 14

A STRONG PURPOSE AND UNDEFEATABLE SPIRIT IN LIFE

"Life should not be a journey to the grave
with the intention of arriving safely in a pretty
and well preserved body, but rather to skid in
broadside in a cloud of smoke, thoroughly used
up, totally worn out, and loudly proclaiming
'Wow! What a Ride!'"
— Hunter S. Thompson, *The Proud Highway:*
Saga of a Desperate Southern Gentleman

It was a hot summer day. A young labourer woman, Falguni, left home carrying lunch for her labourer husband, who was working in the fields but she had no idea that she would never reach her destination.

She had to climb a mountain to reach him, but unfortunately, her foot slipped and she fell from the mountain. Her husband kept waiting for his lunch. When he was told about the accident, he ran to his wife frantically. He wasted no time and took his beloved wife to the hospital, which was fifty-five kilometres away, but by the time they reached, she had already left the world.

He blamed the mountain for his loss and decided to break it and make a path through it so that other people from his village could get medical help on time. After all, the mountain was the reason why it took him so long to go to the hospital as it obstructed the path from his village to the hospital and therefore people had to take a long route to reach there. The death of his wife filled the poor man with a strong purpose in life and an undefeatable spirit. He took a hammer and a chisel and started the impossible mission of breaking the mountain. After twenty-two years of hard work, he managed to carve out a 360 feet long, 30 feet high, and 30 feet wide passage through the mountain single-handedly. He shortened the fifty-five kilometres' distance to fifteen kilometres so that no one from his village would ever lose a wife, a child, a father, a mother, or a husband because of the delay in reaching the hospital. This man's name was Dashrath Manjhi, and he was given the title 'The Mountain Man' after his death in the village in Bihar, India, where he lived. But Dashrath Manjhi is not the only person who found a strong purpose in life after seeing the death of a loved one.

If we read newspapers and history, we will find many examples of people who decided to do something magnificent after seeing death from very close quarters and becoming strongly aware of it. When we realise that we as well as our loved ones are not immortal, many times we feel a strong desire to make our lives meaningful and significant. And when we truly understand that we have to lose everything one day, we are no longer afraid of failure and losing things in the pursuit of our goals. But we don't have to wait for this motivation till we lose somebody we love. The exercises to develop an awareness of death are enough to make us feel the shortness of time we have.

In addition, you can do this little experiment to find out your true purpose. Whenever you get a spare hour, sit with a piece of paper and write down a few paragraphs on things that give you a strong purpose in life. This experiment will work only if you are ready to go deep into your mind and honestly ask yourself about these things. Very few of us will be lucky enough to write it perfectly within an hour. Most of us might need a few weeks, a few months, or maybe a few years to find out those things. But this one hour can be the first step in the long journey of self-exploration. And once you are able to write down those things, you will feel a surge of energy and determination to seek them. This experiment will be more powerful if you keep reminding yourself that despite all the life-enhancing drugs and anti-ageing creams, your time on the earth is very short. Very soon, you will be wiped out from this world. Thus, you can't waste it in dilly-dallying and doing meaningless things if you want deep satisfaction and a sense of purposefulness.

Once we understand this, we will start looking for something which fulfils us, which gives us the nectar of deep satisfaction. We don't have to do something as gigantic as carving a path through mountains. It can be as small as taking care of a stray animal or doing something which adds small value to somebody's life. But whatever we choose to do will come from our inner depths and it will have our inner strength. In other words, the realisation of the finiteness of life can fill us with infinite willpower and a strong purpose. This not only makes our mind stronger but also brings about a change in our heart as well. Let's find out how this happens in the next chapter.

Chapter 15

More Compassion, Less Grudges

*"Death is a challenge. It tells us not to waste
time. It tells us to tell each
other right now that we love each other."*
— Leo Buscaglia

A few years back, I got a chance to go to a huge hospital in Delhi because a friend of mine was getting his father treated and I wanted to assist them. I was waiting in the corridor of the hospital while they were inside the cabin of a doctor to get his prescription. I was feeling sleepy sitting on a chair, and then suddenly I was woken up by the ear-piercing cry of a woman.

I got up, followed the direction of the voice and I found myself in a hall. A woman in her mid-forties was crying hoarsely as if she had lost everything. Around two dozen people had surrounded her and were watching her with a silent expression. Two or three people, who were probably her family members, were trying to console her, but her sorrow was uncontrollable. I watched her with a gloomy face for many minutes, and then I headed back towards my chair. This woman had lost somebody she loved, and she was never going to get that person back. Her sadness and helplessness won't make a difference to the event which cannot be undone.

I sat back and started thinking about that woman. I felt deep compassion and sympathy for her. But then I thought that she wasn't the only one who would be experiencing this grim reality of life. Everyone who has come to this earth will face the loss of his loved ones at least once in life. That person will cry, either silently or loudly, and his sadness won't bring his loved one back. And then I started feeling compassion for everybody on the earth, even for those people whom I disliked. I realised that sorrow comes to all of us, whether we are good people or bad people,

whether we are rich or poor, whether we are young or old. That's what the awareness of death does to us. It makes us understand that we all are slowly inching towards our death and soon, we all will become old and frail and diseased. We will cry for our loved ones, and our loved ones will cry for us. That's a law of nature and it doesn't have a single exception. And it's not going to see an exception in our lives too.

The compassion which arises from seeing the death of somebody intimate is so immense among some people that they also forgive those people who murdered their dear ones. In 2018, the old mother of Fr. Xavier Thelekkat forgave the murderer of her son who had killed him after being fired for his alcoholism during work. She understood the suffering of the family members of the murderer and hugged his wife with love. In 2017, the father of a pizza delivery driver forgave and embraced the man who was an accomplice in the murder of his son. Abdul-Munim Sombat Jitmoud hugged the defendant and said he forgave him because God won't be able to forgive the accused if he didn't forgive him first.

It makes us understand that compassion and grudges cannot stay in the same heart. They are like water and fire and hence they cannot simultaneously coincide. And once we start understanding the pain that we all go through, we would not want to add more pain in anyone's life.

Remember that within fifty years, most of the people we know will be old or dead. Our well-wishers and our tormentors—all will be lying in the dust. We don't need to be a genius to figure out what will make us happier in these years—a heart filled with compassion or a heart exploding with grudges.

And as we discover the joy of compassion, let's see how we can get inspired to continue living on this earth even after our death in an innovative way.

Chapter 16

RISE OF THE CREATIVE GIANT
SLEEPING INSIDE US

"We fear death, we shudder at life's instability,
we grieve to see the flowers wilt again and
again, and the leaves fall, and in our hearts
we know that we, too, are transitory and will
soon disappear. When artists create pictures
and thinkers search for laws and formulate
thoughts, it is in order to salvage something
from the great dance of death, to make
something last longer than we do."
— Hermann Hesse, *Narcissus and Goldmund*

*I*t was not an easy day for the young writer. He had spent the last few months of his life in a prison that contained his country's most vicious and cruel criminals. As if being interrogated by the toughest army personnel every day was not enough, now he was condemned to be shot by the firing squad along with his friends. And what was his crime?

He was a part of the group of artists and thinkers who discussed ideas like equality and justice and read thought-provoking books. He was also accused of writing and propagating letters that talked about rebellion against the existing king and his way of ruling people. And obviously, the king didn't want to have any kind of revolution in his country which could overthrow him and, maybe, end his life.

Finally, the day of execution arrived for the writer. It was a cold December and the temperature was freezing. He was wearing the same clothes which he had put on six months back while being arrested in his apartment and hounded like animals. He felt his death was just a few minutes away. He imagined that now he will hear gunshots and within a fraction of a second, he will feel bullets pierce his chest and end his life. A part of his mind was hoping that he would be saved somehow, and if that happened, he was sure that he won't waste even a single moment of his life again. He promised to himself that his life will become endless, a whole eternity, and he will live differently. He saw his friends standing in front of gunmen and waiting for the trigger to be pulled. After them, it would be his turn. Wait for a few minutes and everything would be over. And then suddenly, a carriage came into the square, and a man came out with a message from the king—their death sentences were commuted. The young writer was going to live. He was given a second chance at life.

He spent the next few years toiling in a secluded place under the most abysmal prison conditions and a stint in the army. But he never forgot what he had promised to himself while praying for an escape from death. He thought about the time he had spent in error and idleness. He was not going to do it anymore, and he was going to spend every minute of his life creating masterpieces that would live for centuries after him. He was not given any writing tools, so he wrote in his mind. He created characters, scenes, story plots, chapters, and book structures on his mental screen while he was working day and night as a part of the punishment. He made a pledge to himself that he would try to get as much as possible in the shortest time. The close encounter with death had aroused an intense awareness in him which had made him insanely focussed towards his goal. He had learnt his time was extremely limited on the planet and he was not going to squander even a second of it.

We all have heard the name of this writer—Fyodor Dostoevsky. That awareness of death catapulted him into becoming one of the best novelists of the world and motivated him to create classic masterpieces like *Crime and Punishment*, *The Brothers Karamazov*, and many others. But I forgot to tell you one important part of the story: that death sentence was not real. It was a scary prank played by the Russian king, Tsar Nicholas I, to infuse the terror of death among people who were trying to rebel against him. When Dostoevsky was counting his last moments, he was not actually in real danger. Without his knowledge, he was imagining his death which felt as real as facing the real death. And that's the whole point of doing some of the awareness of death exercises we have discussed in Part II of the book.

As mentioned before, when we imagine our death and feel its ferociousness to our deepest core, we realise we are not here on this planet for a very long time. And this realisation can also spark an immense amount of creativity in us. But why? What does creativity have to do with our mortality? That's a natural and very good question. So, when we come face to face with our imminent death, when we realise that very soon we won't be on this earth, many of us would want to continue living on this earth through something we leave here, and one of the things we can leave on this planet is some creative work. This is how awareness of death can propel creativity.

Won't it be nice if we can leave a book, a painting, a poem, a movie, a sculpture, a discovery, an invention, or anything else which reminds people of us after we are gone? For many of us, it might seem like a wonderful idea. It's a symbolic immortality we would like to attain and which might motivate the creativity lying inside us to wake up and realise its full potential.

Most of the people who have lived will be forgotten after their demise, but we will always remember the great artists, writers, scientists, thinkers, and other innovators who have left something valuable on earth before saying the final goodbye. This includes people like Shakespeare, Newton, Kalidasa, Rumi, Leonardo Da Vinci, the Buddha, Christ, and countless others who lived on this earth and created something significant. But what if we can't create a masterpiece like Mona Lisa or Meghadootam or Calculus? The truth is that it hardly matters what we create. What matters is the fact that we have decided to make the best of every waking moment by creating something which will outlast us. This would give us more happiness and contentment than living an uncreative life which is spent in eating, drinking, sleeping, gossiping, and wondering which mindless entertainment to watch in order to spend our leisure time.

So, let's confront our mortality and let it inspire us to create something wonderful which won't die with our death. And while we are creating something wonderful for the world, let's not forget to learn from a great sculptor how to sculpt a beautiful life.

Chapter 17

KNOWLEDGE OF WHAT TRULY MATTERS IN LIFE

"No one ever said on their deathbed, 'Gee, I wish I had spent more time alone with my computer.'"

— Danielle Berry

In the fifteenth century, there lived a talented sculptor in Italy who used to create amazing masterpieces with rocks and his chisel. Give him a huge rock and a few months to work on it, and he could dazzle you with a beautiful statue which could beat all your most wonderful imaginations. One day, somebody asked him, "When I see a rock, I cannot see anything except a rock in it. But you can turn it into a masterpiece. How do you manage to do it?"

The sculptor thought for a minute, analysed his creative process, and replied, "Oh, it's simple. I take the rock and just remove the unnecessary parts which don't have anything to do with the statue."

The art of living a meaningful life is not much different from the way that renowned artist, Michelangelo, created sculptures. We just need to remove those parts of life which don't matter and we need to give our entire attention to the things which are of value and add meaning to our lives. The human life we are given is a huge rock. We are the sculptor. Awareness of death is our chisel. By using awareness of death to get rid of those things which don't matter, very soon we will be left with a meaningful and satisfying life which primarily consists of only those things that matter to us.

Another thing to note is that this talented sculptor never created the same statue twice. The reason being that every rock contained a unique statue in it which had nothing to do with another rock. Similarly, the life of every individual carries a unique statue of a meaningful life. So, the definition of necessary and unnecessary parts will also vary from person to person. What others find necessary for themselves may not be necessary for us, and what we find necessary for us may not be necessary for others. So, it's useless to blindly copy others' preferences and it's more sensible to use the chisel of awareness of death to carve out our own unique meaningful life which is lying hidden in the human life we have been given.

Some people might find that a successful career makes their lives meaningful, so they will pay extra attention to it. Some people might find that a happy family gives them a sense of meaning, so they will make it a priority. Some people might want to do social work, some people might want to create something beautiful, and some people might find meaning in their spiritual growth. But most of us will find a combination of two or three things that will make our lives meaningful. Once we figure out what is truly important, it would be easier for us to discard what doesn't matter to make time for what truly matters.

Many times, we would find that what truly matters and what we truly want (as discussed in Chapter 10) are the same things, and there's nothing surprising in that. But sometimes, we would also see that we don't feel any desire or motivation to pursue what truly matters in our life. In that case, awareness of death can help in creating the motivation and the sense of urgency to do them.

In one of the earlier chapters, we had done the exercise of finding out the most important things to do if we had one day or one month or one year or ten years to live. In this exercise, you would have noticed that our answers start changing as our time frame starts increasing. I feel that when we have a smaller time frame to decide what truly matters, we get more correct answers. The chisel of awareness of death gets sharper if we imagine that our death is closer to us.

The process of chiselling out the unnecessary things in our life can be quite tiresome. We have become so used to doing unnecessary things that they have become an inseparable emotional need for us. We have almost convinced ourselves that we are doing them because we cannot live without them. For example, a friend of mine was telling me that he couldn't say no to any social invitations because he didn't want to offend anybody and spoil relationships although he wanted to spend more time working on a business idea which was very important for him. But when he sat down in solitude and asked himself about the most important thing he would like to do if he had got only one year to live, his priorities became crystal clear to him. He realised that he would prefer to work on his idea than to accept every social invitation that was not helping him in any way. He ended up offending some people for some time, but very soon, they got used to his 'no' and didn't bother him much after that.

So, let's learn from the great sculptor and pick up our chisel to remove all that's unnecessary and carve out a life full of things that truly matter. And then our next step would be to see how we can live in a way that we can leave something behind for others.

Chapter 18

THE URGE TO LEAVE SOMETHING BEHIND BEFORE WE LEAVE

*"What we have done for ourselves alone dies
with us; what we have done for others and the
world remains and is immortal."*

— Albert Pike

The famous movie actor and humourist Woody Allen had said, "I don't want to achieve immortality through my work. I want to achieve it through not dying." Many of us would agree with the honesty in this witty quote. We don't want to die and that's why we have a flourishing pharmaceutical industry, nutritional food and dieting industry, cosmetic industry, hospital sector, etc. Our entire effort is focused towards elongating our physical life as much as possible. But the bad news is that eventually, we all will die. Thankfully, here we have good news too. We can keep living in this world through something we leave behind even if we are not as creative as Woody Allen.

In 1888, an extremely rich Swedish man opened the newspaper and read something that none of us will ever get to read in our lifetime—one's own obituary. It had been published by a French newspaper by mistake. The obituary had described in extremely bitter words the demise of the 'merchant of death' who had become filthy rich by developing new ways to mutilate and kill. He couldn't believe that he would be remembered in this way by the world after his death and thus decided to do something about it. He called up his assistant to prepare a document that will make him immortal in the memory of the world in a desirable way.

On November 27, 1895, this 62-year-old industrialist signed his last will and testament at Paris' Swedish-Norwegian Club. This document described a project to promote scientists, inventors, writers, and peace workers in a way that was never done before by anybody. In a small write-up of less than 1000 words, this gentleman had outlined a plan to devote almost 94 per cent of his assets—worth around $265 million today—to a series of annual prizes for "those who, during the preceding year, shall have conferred the greatest benefit on mankind."

This industrialist was successful at his attempt of becoming immortal through his work and is now a household name today. Today, we don't remember him as the 'dynamite king' who manufactured and sold explosives that were used in wars to kill people but rather as a servant of humanity who donated his wealth to promote literature, scientific inventions, economic theories, and world peace by giving the most prestigious award in the world in his name.

Most of us are not as rich as Alfred Nobel and probably we would never be rich enough to start something like Nobel Prize in our name. But it doesn't mean that we cannot leave some legacy behind us which will make us immortal in the eyes of the world even after we are gone. We can be the poorest man on this earth and still leave something on this planet which will keep on living after us for decades or centuries. In Chapter 13, we have discussed the story of a daily labourer who carved a path through a hill so that the people from his village could reach the hospital faster. But again, we don't have to undertake a gigantic task like breaking a mountain to help the world. We can find our own thing which we love doing and we would like to contribute to the world.

A good way to find out your passion is by learning from the event that changed the life course of Alfred Nobel—reading his own obituary. So, what if we write our own obituary? The reason for this is that it will make you

contemplate an important question: How would you like to be remembered by the world including your family, friends, and others who know you?

You can write one or two small paragraphs as your obituary or you can also write a full essay with all the necessary details, if you feel so. To make your obituary more insightful, you can also ask your close friends and family members to advise you. Although many of them would be shocked to hear this weird request from you, some of them would definitely help you in a good spirit. Through this, you will get to know:

- How do they see us?
- How would they like to remember us?
- What are the qualities which will make us unforgettable to them?
- Would they like to remember us in some specific way?

But more importantly, they can advise us to do something according to our abilities which will make us leave a wonderful legacy. The Anglo-American writer, Susan Ertz, had said, "Millions long for immortality who don't know what to do with themselves on a rainy Sunday afternoon." Maybe we can spend those rainy Sunday afternoons devoting ourselves to pursue and create something which might give us a flavour of immortality. But just by idly fantasising about immortality in spare time and doing nothing about it won't take us anywhere. We need to take a major step like the character of Mr Kanji Watanbe in the great Japanese movie, Ikiru, which was directed by Akira Kurosawa in 1952.

Kanji had been living a monotonous and meaningless life for thirty years as a bureaucrat when his doctors discovered that he had stomach cancer and only had a few months to live. This sudden confrontation with the inevitable death made him question the way he had been living, and he decided to build a children's park in a poor slum neighbourhood. He surmounted every difficulty which came in his path and met his death with a peaceful demeanour after completing this park and leaving something behind for small children. In the Japanese language, 'Ikiru' means to live. Kanji learnt to live when he knew that his life would be over soon.

Kanji was a fictional character, but we will find plenty of examples of people in the real world who also learnt to live after being in a situation where they couldn't postpone life anymore. Let's look at our own life. We also don't know how much time we have got to live. It's better to start living right now with full intensity and a strong desire to leave something behind which could be as small as a fruit tree or as big as a world-class prize.

The famous poet, Rabindranath Tagore, had written, "The one who plants trees, knowing that he will never sit in their shade, has at least started to understand the meaning of life." Let's plant a tree and keep living through its shade which will give comfort and joy to the generations to come.

While we get busy doing something we can leave behind for others, we shouldn't forget to impress that person who matters most to us. Many of us end up ignoring that person because we are too busy seeking the approval of others. Let's see how we can avoid this mistake.

Chapter 19

A Stronger Desire to Impress Ourselves

"If you know how quickly people forget the dead, you will stop living to impress people."
— Christopher Walken

"My father was the editor-in-chief of one of the biggest newspapers of the country. When he died, the next day the newspaper company cancelled the free subscription of the newspaper at our home." This line by a stand-up comedian, whose name I don't remember, amuses us by showing a scathing reality of life. When somebody dies, most people forget him too quickly and move on. The world rarely stops to mourn the dead or show concern for the near and dear ones of the deceased person.

But what do we do? We spend our entire life trying to impress the world and seeking its approval in most of the matters of our life. We try to look good, successful, generous, smart, rich, and one hundred other things in the eyes of the people who will forget us within a minute of our departure. And, frankly speaking, we will also forget most of the people we know within an hour of their death. It's a two-way street.

The seeds of this deep desire to impress others are sown very early in our childhood when our parents and teachers unknowingly teach us that we must always worry about what others think about us. Our worth starts getting judged by what others think and say about us. Although this teaching has some practical benefits and it is helpful to look good in the eyes of society, but the problem starts when this desire becomes an obsession and starts guiding most of our decisions of life. We start ignoring what we really want and start doing things that can bring us the acceptance and approval of others. Slowly, we completely forget what our inner desires and convictions are and only care about how we appear in others' opinions.

I remember an insightful story by Khalil Gibran. Somebody asked a scarecrow, "You must be tired of standing in this lonely field."

The scarecrow replied, "The joy of scaring is a deep and lasting one, and I never tire of it."

Then that person said, "It is true for I too have known that joy."

The scarecrow replied, "Only those who are stuffed with straw can know it."

We too have lost a lot of our real essence and filled ourselves with straws. Just like the scarecrow enjoys scaring others to feel happy, we try to create a powerful impression on others to feel good. Many times, we would even prefer to look fake to impress others than to be real to impress ourselves. This fakeness has become such an inseparable part of ourselves that we don't see anything wrong with that. Then we wonder why we feel so much discontentment and unhappiness in life and why we feel so empty inside.

But when we develop an awareness of death and feel the closeness and inevitability of our demise, we realise that we have very little time and we cannot afford to waste it doing things that don't give us real happiness. And when we realise how quickly people would forget us after we are gone, we start preferring to do things we would want to do rather than what others would want us to do. We start losing the force of peer pressure on our psyche and also stop wondering whether we are following the latest fashion trend or not. We don't feel the compulsion to read or watch a particular thing just because it's considered to be cool to talk about it. We no longer compare ourselves with others on every parameter and stop using others' eyes as a mirror to see how we look, how we live, and how successful we are. We realise that we have enough time only to do the essentials, and those essentials come from our real needs and inner convictions. This realisation of the impermanence of life will make us ask what are those things that will truly impress us. We start seeking our inner compass rather than following others' signboards. This way we will also get a taste of real freedom which comes from breaking the invisible shackles of others' opinions and judgments and this, in turn, will inspire us to fly high in the sky before we lie under the earth. Remember that it's better to impress that one person we have to live with day and night than to try to impress one thousand others who are too busy with their own lives.

Now it's time to find out how this desired awareness can make us focused towards the most important element of life.

Chapter 20

FEELING CLOSER TO OUR LOVED ONES

"It is a curious thing, the death of a loved one.
We all know that our time in this world is
limited, and that eventually all of us will end
up underneath some sheet, never to wake up.
And yet it is always a surprise when it happens
to someone we know. It is like walking up
the stairs to your bedroom in the dark, and
thinking there is one more stair than there is.
Your foot falls down, through the air, and there
is a sickly moment of dark surprise as you try
and readjust the way you thought of things."
— Lemony Snicket, *Horseradish*

A famous doctor has spent a big part of his career being with patients who were close to death. He talks about a significant difference he observed in the ways of thinking of those who felt they were not close to death and those who felt they were nearing their end.

Those who felt they were far away from death generally had big money and career goals. They wanted to build networks with people, work hard in their profession, and earn more money and prestige. On the other hand, those who realised they were near their death wanted to spend the remaining part of their lives with their loved ones. They wanted to be with their family members, close friends, and others they loved. Here comes the more interesting part. The same people who felt they were near their death, when given the option of a new medicine or medical treatment that will elongate their life span, automatically changed their priorities and wanted to spend more time on their career rather than with their family. The thing to note here is that there is a very strong connection between our priorities in life and how much time we think we have in our life. When we have less time, we seek more love and when we have more time, we seek more materialistic success. And since most of us think that we have lots of time on the earth, we tend to give more importance to the materialistic success part.

Let me share an observation with which you might also agree. I have seen a very common reaction among the family members and friends of a person who has left the earth recently. They complain and regret that they didn't get enough time to spend with that person and they wish that the person should have lived for a few years more. Surprisingly, they give the same reaction even if the person happened to be very old. This makes me wonder how much time is enough for a person to live on this earth so that others feel that they have got enough time to spend with him or her. Is it seventy years, eighty years, ninety years, or even more? I don't think there is any definite answer for that. And even if there was a definite answer, there is no guarantee from life that a person would be able to touch that age boundary.

Well, let's assume that there was an absolute guarantee that we are going to live on this earth for the next fifty years.

Then it would have been a good strategy to spend forty years in making a fabulous amount of money and spending the last five or ten years in sharing love with our dear ones. But, as we discussed before, here we have a problem. There is no certainty about how much time we will get to spend in this physical body. While I am writing this chapter, I am not sure if I will be alive to write the next one. Life can be that unpredictable. But this doesn't mean that we should ignore our career, stop making money, and refuse to seek material comforts. We need financial security in life, and we must work hard enough to gain it. Instead, the thing we need to understand is that our time on the planet is short and it may not be very wise to sacrifice love and affection to get simply ahead in materialistic success. We should give balanced importance to both, a career as well as love.

When I had joined an advertising agency after finishing college, my well-intentioned boss advised me to forget my family and friends to focus completely on my career. He also suggested that I should be ready to sacrifice my holidays, hobbies, and other activities in life so that I could become 'successful' like him. He meant the best for me and was just talking honestly about what being successful meant to him. But the awareness of death gave me a different perspective. It urged me to find out my own definition of success which came from my inner self rather than from the well-to-do careerists, the popular definition of success, motivational gurus, society, and trends in fashion. It motivated me to become successful in my own heart rather than in others' eyes.

When we practice the exercises to develop an awareness of death, we will find our own idea of success, but I doubt that our idea of success will ignore what really matters in life, which is love. And as we become more and more aware of our mortality, we can ask ourselves if it's really worthwhile to slog day and night in the workplace so that we can add a few more zeroes to our bank accounts. Also, we won't be able to take our money with us after death or transfer it to our next birth. When our eyes close forever, we cannot take even a coin with us. So, what's the point in earning and accumulating far more than we would ever need? My personal observation has been that many of us earn and accumulate far more than we need because deep inside, we fear our death, and we think that a big amount of money will save us from dying. The added zeroes in our bank account give us a false sense of security, and we keep chasing that mirage of security our whole life.

But once we face our mortality and accept the biggest fear, we don't need the illusion of security that money and materialistic success promise to give. Instead, we start looking for the real satisfaction that only love and affection give us. With this realisation, we won't spend our free time going for a drink with our boss or colleagues so that we can build more professional contacts. On the contrary, we would spend that time with people we genuinely love and cherish.

Here I would like to again make myself clear that I am not advocating against building a good career. All I am saying is that if we are aware of the shortness and unpredictability of life, things driven by love will become more important to us than the things driven by our ego. We also need to make the definition of 'loved ones' a little wider. Under this category, along with the people we love, we can also add the things and activities we love. Many great artists, writers, innovators, mystics, scientists, and other creators may not have spent much time with their family or friends, but they spent their time generously with the things they loved doing. Their fascination with work was not an ego trip for more money, prestige, and accumulations; it came from a pure love of creating something wonderful for their creative satisfaction and the benefit of the world.

As we put more focus on the things we love, we can take care of one very important thing that can make a big difference. When we spend time with our loved ones, we should work more towards increasing the intensity of our presence rather than the length of duration. Let me explain

BE FULLY PRESENT WHILE
TALKING TO YOUR MOM.
THAT'S THE BEST PRESENT
YOU CAN GIVE TO HER.

it a bit more. In a span of twenty-four hours, we have to take care of many responsibilities and that's why, on many occasions, we won't be able to give more time to our loved ones. But we can do another thing. We can try to be fully present with them whenever we get time to spend with them. We can avoid checking our phones, watching TV, or doing something else while we talk to them and give our complete attention to them. We can treat them as if they are the most important person on the earth, and frankly speaking, they are the most important person on the earth for us in that moment. When we are with them, we should be completely there with them.

Thus, it's better to spend half hour with full presence than to spend three hours where other things are stealing a major part of our attention. It will automatically enhance the depth of our conversation and we will be able to express our feelings more and feel more satisfied with the experience. And if we do this, we will regret less that we didn't get more time to spend with a person. After all, it's not the duration which matters; it's the intensity of our interaction which matters more. And our full presence with the person will ensure a great intensity in our interactions.

One of the beautiful lessons from death is that it teaches us how to give importance to love, and its awareness softly pushes us closer to the people and things we really love. It makes us realise that only love can make every moment of this earthly life complete.

Now it's time to learn how we can reduce the mental suffering of those who are going through an immense amount of trauma and are unable to share their feelings with others at the most critical time of their lives.

Chapter 21

BEING A GREAT FRIEND TO PEOPLE ON DEATHBED

*"With those people who are actually dying,
it's good if the surrounding people have some
knowledge [of how to help]. As I mentioned
earlier, with those dying people who believe in
a creator god, you can remind them of God.
A single-pointed faith in God has at least
some benefit, from a Buddhist point of view
as well. With those people who have no belief,
no religion, then as I mentioned earlier, be
realistic, and it's important to try to keep their
minds calm."*

— Dalai Lama, *Advice on Dying: And Living a
Better Life*

I can never forget the day when I saw my lovely grandma lying in a bed—old and frail and a few days away from her departure from the world. It was also my first experience to see somebody writhing with pain in the final days of their life and it taught me something that I will never forget.

While most of us were trying our best to give her the medical help and personal care she needed, we never tried to accept the fact verbally that it was time for her to go. A slight smile on her face made us assume that she was recovering and very soon she will leave the bed and start walking on the earth like nothing had happened. There were people who had transformed themselves into medical experts and tried telling others that her face says that she is getting better. But deep inside, we all knew that she won't survive. And I think she also knew that her time was up, yet nobody said it on the face. Talking about death is considered to be so negative and inauspicious in our society that we put this fact of life under a thick carpet and pretend that it doesn't exist.

I don't know what my grandma was going through at that time but I can make a wild guess: she was suffering from great physical and emotional pain. And what do we want to do when we are suffering from some emotional pain? We want to talk about it with somebody who can listen and understand and show some genuine empathy. My grandma wanted the same. She wanted to have a heart-to-heart and honest conversation with the people she knew and loved. It might not have saved her from death, but it might have given her a peaceful departure from the world. But how could she talk about her situation with people who simply didn't want to accept her reality? How could she share things honestly with people who had decided to deny her imminent demise? Thus, she kept her emotions inside and kept suffering from the pent-up feelings and eventually, she died alone on a ventilator after a few days.

This is not just the story of my late grandma; this is the story of millions of people who are lying hopelessly on hospital beds, surrounded by medical equipment and professional healthcare workers who can do something about their physical ailments but cannot do a single thing about their emotional pain. This is also going to be the story of most of us too, who are healthy right now but will find themselves in a similar situation one day for sure. And if we don't learn how to develop an awareness of death and if we don't accept its inevitability, we also are going to multiply our sufferings.

Now let's imagine that my grandma had at least one person in her proximity who had a more honest and mature approach towards death, who didn't hide this reality under a carpet, and who could listen and understand her emotional pain with infinite patience and empathy. If this was the case, then her last days on the earth would have been different. Her physical pain won't have subsided for sure, but she would have felt much better sharing her deep emotions, thoughts, and anguish. This would have allowed her to share her fear of death and the unknown path she would have to travel after that. This would have invited her to share what she felt about people that were close to her and what she wanted to tell them before she left. And most importantly, this would have made her accept that it's time to go and that acceptance would have brought her great mental peace. But no! Nothing like that happened and nothing like that happens in the last days of most of the people. You can blame it on our escapist attitude towards death which is common in most parts of the world.

A great man once said that we should be the change we want to see in the world. So, when we start developing the awareness of death, we start becoming the change we want to see all around us. We can be the person with whom a dying person can share whatever he or she wants to share without the fear of being refused, judged, or ignored. We can be that pleasant exception for such people. And believe me, we will also be rewarded generously when we will reach a hospital bed after some time. Since we have practised facing our death so many times, we will suffer less on the emotional level and we will have a peaceful mind which will be okay with our departure and starting a new journey.

Here I would like to share a Buddhist meditation called Tonglen to increase our compassion and reduce the suffering of those who are ill or dying or in some other kind of pain. We can do it while sitting with the person or we can also do it at some place where we feel peaceful. Its technique is very simple.

- STEP 1: Sit or lie quietly and get comfortable. Start taking many slow and deep breaths. It will make you relaxed and calm.

- STEP 2: Close your eyes. Imagine the person that you want to help. It can be a person on their deathbed. It can also be the person who has already died or is going through some other kind of pain. Focus on that person and on their struggle and feel their pain.

- STEP 3: Slowly take a deep breath and focus on their negative energy and things that trouble them. Imagine yourself breathing in their pain and suffering. You can also visualise their pain in the form of black smoke which you are taking inside. Visualise that as the black smoke is leaving their body and entering your nostrils, they are feeling peaceful and relaxed.

- STEP 4: Breathe out and as you do it, imagine that white smoke is coming out of your nose and entering their body. That white smoke contains peace and joy. Imagine that the white smoke is filling their body with comfort and happiness.

- STEP 5: Repeat. Continue this practice of breathing in pain and breathing out peace over and over again for many minutes. You can also do it for half an hour or more, several times a day.

It's worth pointing that we don't need to be a Buddhist or a religious person to get the benefits of this technique just like we don't need to be a Hindu to get the health benefits of yoga. This technique can benefit everybody and we don't need any kind of faith to see its results. We can also teach this technique to the person who is on the deathbed if they are open to it. It will reduce their mental suffering too.

In a famous book on Tibetan Buddhism, a teacher talks about a young cancer patient who felt very sad and frustrated in the last months of his life. He also felt his life was meaningless. After practising this technique many times, he became full of compassion and felt his life was worthy of something because he was alleviating others' sufferings. Remember that nobody needs a considerate friend more than the person who awaits his demise. The awareness of death can turn us into that friend.

In the next chapter, we will explore how we can come out of the pressure to be constantly competitive and learn to relax with ourselves.

Chapter 22

HUMILITY IN, EGO OUT

*"Humility is a strange thing. Once you think
you have got it, you have lost it."*
— Sir Edward Hulse

For many of us, humility is not an inner virtue we carry. It's a social mask we wear. We understand that if we pretend to have humility, we will be liked more by people, we will have better relationships with them, and we can also convince others to do the things we want them to do. Arrogance is generally disliked by people and it backfires some or the other day, and that's why we decide to look modest. But what we fail to realise is that the pretension of humility has negative effects.

One can say that pretentious humility looks like a bad plastic surgery on a face. It forces us to show a fake behaviour pattern all the time which, in turn, creates mental stress. It becomes a trick by the ego to create a pleasant and desirable image in society, but it also has the disadvantages that a big and insidious ego brings.

Beneath the mask of humility, we remain the same person who is easily hurt by others' unpleasant comments, who is always under the pressure to prove that he is better than others, and who has to always stay careful that his mask is not taken away from him. But if we have made the necessary effort to develop an awareness of death, we won't have to worry about developing fake humility. When we realise that everything we are so proud of can be taken away and will certainly be taken away, we spontaneously develop true humility which comes from the knowledge that actually we have nothing to be so egoistic about.

Whenever I go to my ancestral home, I see the pictures of my grandparents hanging on the walls. Till a few years back, they were alive and they were living the lives just like we are living right now. But now, they are gone. Their entire generation has vanished. They lived on the earth for more than eighty years. They made money, built houses, fought with people for dominance, tried to believe that the world needs them desperately, worried about million things, and felt that they would live forever. But now there is no trace left of them except in some old photographs hanging on the walls. New generations have come to the planet and one by one, they will also disappear from earth after some time.

We will also meet the same fate. After a few decades, most of us will stay in the world only through some old photographs and occasional conversations among the newer generations. So, what's there to be so proud about? What's there to be so egoistic about? What's there to make us feel that we are so important to the world?

We are like the water from a river that comes and goes and the world is like the bank of that river which will always stay there. The bank neither worries about water that has passed by nor does it keep a record of water that has left. The bank knows that the present water will go away and new water will keep coming. But we try to behave like water which wants to stay forever. Our ego pushes us to try hard to gain the importance in the eyes of the world we actually don't possess. The awareness of death gives a hard time to this ego and stops it from imposing its importance on the world.

Ego is like a balloon that is effortlessly pricked by the needle of our mortality. And when we become strongly aware of our mortality, we get a taste of genuine humility which comes from the knowledge about how vulnerable we are. The beauty of inculcating genuine modesty is that it also brings invaluable benefits. So far, we had been stressed by the persistent demands of ego. And just like a glutton needs food all the time, our ego needs consistent fuel every hour of the day. That's why we are always looking for attention and appreciation from others. We always want to be the star of the show no matter how small or big the show is. But when the awareness of death gives us an experience of genuine modesty, we realise how futile our obsession is and how empty our egoistic demands are. The peace and joy that comes from true humility are far better than the momentary excitement and pleasure that come from egoistic satisfaction.

Also, with this genuine humility, we will experience that the key to our happiness lies with us. So far, due to the demands of the ego, we had handed over the key to our happiness to others. If they said we are good, we felt happy. If they said we are bad, we felt unhappy. If they gave attention to us, we felt good. If they didn't give attention to us, we felt bad. But when we develop humility, we realise that we don't need the constant supply of attention or validation from others. We lose the persistent desire to look better than others, and we also lose the dependency on others' approval to feel good about ourselves. This makes us relaxed and calm.

From our childhood, we have been taught by our family, teachers, and society to be the best. But we never think why we should try so hard to be the best. Trying to be the best is the demand of our ego, and our society is mostly driven by the needs of the ego. It's not a coincidence that our society is rarely aware of the impending death of human life. But when we, as individuals, become conscious of our death in a healthy way, we feel more motivated by the things which are driven by love rather than the things driven by ego. When love replaces ego, humility becomes the most natural aftermath effect. Then we no longer want to 'be the best' and instead prefer to 'be modest'.

Centuries back, there lived a king in India who was loved by his people for his sense of justice and humility. He also invited learned men to his court to have bold and honest discussions on various topics. They were even allowed to question the actions and behaviour of the king without the fear of any punishment.

One day, a young man participated in the discussion and accused the king of living in excessive luxury and not understanding the plight of people from the unprivileged classes. The king listened to him silently and offered him to sit on his throne and have a direct experience of this 'excessive luxury' he was enjoying. But there was a condition: the young man had to sit on the throne the whole day and he couldn't leave it except for the bathroom and food breaks. The young man took the offer happily.

The next morning, he became the king and sat on the throne. He felt a gush of excitement and ecstasy when he saw that an entire kingdom was under his control. He could give whatever orders he wanted to and enjoy all luxuries by just speaking a few words. While he was diving in the ocean of this amazing thrill, his eyes went to the ceiling and immediately felt as if he was going to have a severe heart attack. There was a sword hanging on a thin thread that was tied to the ceiling. The sword could fall down at any time and cut his skull into two pieces. He tried to get up and run away, but he was forcefully made to sit back on the throne by the soldiers. The king, sitting as a courtier, reminded him of the condition he had accepted while taking the offer.

From this moment on, nobody saw even a glimpse of pleasure and pride on his face. Luckily, the sword didn't fall down and he stayed alive till the evening to get up and relinquish the luxuries of the throne. Then the king explained to him modestly, "Dear young man, that's how I sit every day. You saw the luxuries, but you never noticed the sword. That sword keeps reminding me of the impending death which can come any time. Being a powerful king hardly make me safer than other people on the earth. It also gives me the humility to understand the suffering of my people."

We all have swords hanging on our heads, but we are not aware of them since most of these swords are invisible. The awareness of death makes us realise the presence of these swords because of which we end up developing genuine humility like the king. Resultantly, the pressures of ego are replaced by the peace of modesty.

Now it's time to explore another benefit and find out how we can avoid burying our great ideas, aspirations, and important plans in the fanciest graveyard of the world.

Chapter 23

No More Procrastination

*"Only put off until tomorrow what you are
willing to die having left undone."*
— Pablo Picasso

There is a special day in our life on which we plan to do everything we want to. But the irony is that that day never arrives and we refer to it as 'tomorrow'.

We all have this habit of postponing everything important till tomorrow. If we want to write a book, we want to start tomorrow. If want to work on an idea, we want to take the first step tomorrow. If we want to tell somebody that we love him or her, we want to do it tomorrow. If we want to come out of a bad job or a bad relationship, we want to do it tomorrow.

Have you ever thought that why do we postpone everything to tomorrow? It is because we believe that we have a long life ahead of us and therefore, we will have plenty of time to do whatever we want to do. So, today we can relax and waste our time. But if we have developed at least some awareness of death, we will realise that our dependency on tomorrow is as futile as expecting muscle-building nutrition from a carbonated soft drink. We will recognise the fact we don't have an unlimited number of tomorrows. The truth is that there is no guarantee that tomorrow will come. And even if tomorrow comes, we will find another tomorrow to postpone the important stuff.

Tomorrow is the fancy graveyard where we bury our great ideas, aspirations, expressions of love, and other important things. Tomorrow is the anaesthesia that kills the potential of wonderful things we can do. And by saying 'I will do it tomorrow' allows us to ignore our responsibilities and the guilt that comes from postponing a task indefinitely.

A wise man once said, "The trouble is, you think you have time." Yes, this is the biggest problem we have. We think we have infinite time and our death is very far from us. But we forget that death is a moody prankster and it can raise its head anytime, anywhere. This is a strange predicament of human life. When we are young, we think we have too much time and we can procrastinate. And when we get old, we think we don't have enough time and we cannot do what we want to. But the real fact is that a young person is as far away from death as an old person. The young person doesn't have too much time and the old person doesn't have too little time. Both of them have got only one day to do something and that day is called today.

Let's take the first step today towards whatever we want to do. The good thing is that it doesn't matter how big or small our first step is. A baby would never learn to walk if it decides to take big steps like adults. A painter would never be able to complete a painting if he doesn't want to make the first small stroke required to start making the painting. A chef would never be able to cook delicacies if he avoids taking the small step of burning a stove. Worrying about the first step and not doing it is just a way to camouflage our habit of procrastination. It's okay to keep our first step very small. A small step is all we need to break the habit of procrastination. And if we feel too lazy to take that step today, we must not forget that death has already taken one more step towards us anyway. Unlike us, death never procrastinates. This truth should motivate us to get to what we really want to do.

In the next chapter, we will see how we can find happiness by making the best use of the most precious commodity before it vanishes.

Chapter 24

LIVING IN THE NOW

*"Time isn't precious at all, because it is an
illusion. What you perceive as precious is not
time but the one point that is out of time: the
Now. That is precious indeed. The more you
are focused on time—past and future—the
more you miss the Now, the most precious
thing there is."*

— Eckhart Tolle

*I*n 1895, a great British writer, H. G. Wells, wrote a small
novel titled *The Time Machine,* which became the source
material for many movies, books, TV serials and other
adaptations in the coming century. It is a science fiction
story that experimented with the idea of time and told the
story of a man who could travel into the past or future by
using a special device. Most of us would like to live the life of
that man if given an opportunity. We would like to go back
to our childhood and enjoy playing hide and seek again.
We would like to go into the future and see the results of
the decisions we are taking right now so that we can come
back to the present life and make the necessary changes for
better results.

But what if I tell you that we all carry that device in our
own life and misuse it so much that it never lets us be happy

and content? Yes, I am talking about our mind which acts as a time machine most of the time. It keeps carrying us into the memories of the past and the fantasies of the future again and again. It makes us travel at extraordinary speeds and it can take us thousands of years back or forward within a fraction of a second. But it has got one major problem: it hates being in the present and prefers to live everywhere except in the NOW. This habit of our mind makes it extremely difficult for us to be in the present moment and enjoy the beauty it offers.

When we think that we have too much time on the earth, we fall into the habit of needlessly thinking about the past or imagining the future. We either start getting anxious about things that might go wrong in the coming days or start regretting things we did or we couldn't do. But when we realise that our time is very limited, the same mind makes us focus on the present moment. This is because the mind realises that it cannot continue having its wasteful attitude towards the precious commodity called time.

Let's understand this by using an example. If you have millions of dollars with you, how are you going to spend it? After taking care of your basic needs, you might splurge it on costly items and might become a little reckless. But if you have got only a few hundred dollars, you will spend every dollar carefully because that's all you have. Now let's replace dollars with the hours we have on the earth. If we think we have a very long life to live, we will spend a lot of time on unnecessary things and activities. We will waste a lot of time regretting the past and daydreaming about the future. But if we are aware of our death, we will know that we don't have unlimited hours on this earth, and that's why we will spend every hour carefully with full attention. This will bring us into the present moment, into the NOW.

A few days back, I was talking to my uncle who is in his seventies. Like many other old people, he also loves talking about his past. That day, he was sharing funny stories from his early childhood and it seemed as if he had reached that era of his life. Then I asked him if he felt that his childhood had happened in the distant past or it had happened just some time back. He nodded his head and said that he felt very near to his childhood as if it had happened yesterday. Just think about what he said. He was talking about the things which had happened fifty-sixty years ago, but he felt that they had happened just some time back.

Now think about your childhood. Don't you feel that it had also happened just a few days back? I certainly feel so. That's one of the facets of time. It passes so fast. It passes faster than an arrow, faster than a bullet, and faster than we can catch up with it. The next ten, twenty, or thirty years too will pass very rapidly. They will go away in a blink. Now let's focus on the present moment. Don't you feel that it's passing very fast? One by one, every moment is going by like the compartments of a fast train and becoming a part of our memory. We must enjoy this moment before it vanishes and becomes a part of the past.

There is only one sure shot way to enjoy our life. We must practice being in the present moment. After all, life is nothing but a series of millions of present moments. The awareness of death can bring us and root us in the present moment. In the coming pages, we will learn the great value of little things from a woman who came back to her senses after losing everything in a mini-death experience.

Chapter 25

SAYING 'THANKS' MORE

"Enjoy the little things, for one day you may
look back and realise
they were the big things."
— Robert Brault

$\mathcal{D}$uring my school days, I had read the memoir of a woman, whose name I don't remember, in a popular magazine where she spoke about how the biggest accident of her life became the biggest boon of her life. That woman had met with a big road accident which kept her bedridden for months. The accident was so severe that she lost her ability to see, hear, and speak for many weeks. She kept lying in the bed like a vegetable, feeling extremely depressed and hopeless about her future. She thought that she would never be able to live a normal life again.

Then after weeks of treatment, she slowly started regaining her ability to see. Initially, things looked foggy and she couldn't recognise faces. Everything looked like a blur to her. After a week or two, her eyesight became better and she could recognise faces and objects and letters. Those were the times when even the smallest improvement in her vision made her extremely happy and hopeful. After months, when she was able to see things clearly, she saw a beautiful flower and kept enjoying its beauty for hours in a mesmerised state. Before her accident, she might have seen thousands of flowers, but their beauty didn't give her the joy which this one flower gave. There was nothing special about this flower; it's just that her way of looking at it had changed.

She had similar experiences regarding hearing and speaking. Now the voice of early morning birds and her mother made her immensely happy. When she could hum a song, she felt as if she was in paradise. She shared her entire experience in her small memoir, *Coming Back to Senses*. In that article, she explained how this mini-death actually made her feel alive and understand the value of every little thing in life after losing them for a temporary period. After this incident, she became thankful for all the things life offered to her. She no longer complained about the petty and irritable things because she understood that she shouldn't let them destroy the grand beauty that her life offered.

In the case mentioned above, the woman lost her senses and the world around her temporarily. But a day will come when we will lose everything permanently. We will lose our ability to see, speak, hear, feel, smell, move, and think. We will lose our family, friends, money, phone, bed, clothes, and million other things which give us happiness and comfort.

It won't be incorrect to say that we don't own any of the things we possess. On this earth, we are like a tenant in a fully furnished house who can enjoy things for a while but doesn't own even a single needle or thread. So, what is there to complain about? Isn't life good enough that we have so many things and our physical abilities allow us to enjoy those things? When we are going to lose everything after a while anyway, shouldn't we be thankful that we have them with us for the time being?

Here, I recall a story of a young man who was so frustrated with his life that he wanted to commit suicide. He went to his teacher and expressed his desire. He thought the teacher will give him emotional support and show some sympathy. But the teacher offered him a sharp knife and

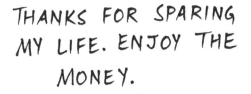

asked him if he would like to donate his eyes, kidneys, and teeth before he ended his life. The young man was shocked to see his teacher's cruel attitude. He told his teacher that his organs were very valuable and he could not give them to anybody. Then the teacher asked him why he wanted to commit suicide if he had such valuable assets. The young man got the point and lost the desire to end his life. He went away with a renewed positivity and energy to live happily.

We all have many valuable assets in life but we don't value them because they are such a common part of our lives that we never wonder how our life would become if we lost them even for a moment. When we meditate on our death, we start understanding the value of those things. We understand they are not going to stay with us forever and so we decide to get as much joy from them as possible. Then we don't look for reasons to complain and instead look for things to be grateful for.

As our next step, we will find out how we can shed our heavy clothes before we dive into the ocean of life for a great swimming experience.

Chapter 26

A Life with Fewer Attachments
and More Freedom

"If you realise that all things change, there is
nothing you will try to hold on to. If you are
not afraid of dying, there is nothing you cannot
achieve."

— Lao Tzu, *Tao Te Ching*

We will start with a small and easy exercise in imagination. Let's imagine that you are working as an employee in an organisation. You fulfil your duties diligently and take care of the furniture given by the organisation to sit and work on. You also take the best care of computers, files, and stationery material provided to perform your job. You enjoy the salary, perks, and other kinds of benefits given by the organisation. You also love the food and coffee in the office canteen. You relish the professional relationships you have developed in the office and try your best to help each other out. You have been given an employee number, an identity card, and an office email id by the administration. And after working there for many years, one day you leave that organisation. Then what will happen to the identity card, employee number, furniture, computer, salary, and other stuff which was given to you by the organisation? You will have to leave everything behind which was given to you to perform your duty. After all, you don't own anything on the premises of that organisation. You were simply an employee and not the owner of the place.

Isn't this scenario very similar to the life we live on the earth? We take birth, we live our lives, we perform our duties, we laugh and cry, we develop relationships, we are given stuff by the world, and then one day, we leave this planet and cannot take away anything with us, not even our body or any of our relationships.

Now let's imagine a different scenario. While working in an organisation, you start believing that you own the place. What will happen after that? So far, the profit or loss of the organisation didn't make much difference to you because you were getting the promised monthly salary. You used the office furniture, canteen, computers, and other things but didn't get disturbed when any of them were malfunctioned or broke down. But now since you have started believing that you own the organisation, every small thing happening there starts affecting you deeply. Even a small loss in the organisation's revenue makes you lose your sleep.

The fact is that this belief of ownership becomes the source of our anxieties and worries. This belief of possessing things makes us very attached to the organisation and we lose the mental peace we had as employees. And a similar thing has happened to our attitude towards our earthly life. We have started believing that we are the owners of the things given by life. We have started assuming that this is our real and permanent home and we will never have to leave this place. This has led to the development of very strong attachments and because of these attachments, we feel very insecure about every little loss in life. We spend sleepless nights worrying over an uncertain future, the loss of our money, prestige, people we love, and the things we cherish.

But the actual facts are completely different. During our exercises to develop an awareness of death, we have seen clearly that in reality, we don't own even a single thing. While visualising our corpse at the cremation ground, we have seen ourselves leaving everything behind—our family, our body, our money, our career, our clothes, our dreams, our aspirations, and our name. In other words, we are not the owners of our life, but we are trying very hard to believe that we own things.

I would like to share a small story to make this point more clear. Once upon a time, a monk came to meet a king. When the monk reached the palace's door, he asked the guard to tell the king that he has come to meet him. The king didn't show any interest in meeting the monk because he was busy with his booze and dancing girls.

When the guard told the monk that the king had no interest in meeting him, the monk shouted so loudly that the king could hear his voice, "Ask the tenant that I want to meet him and I won't go away before having a chat with him." The word 'tenant' infuriated the king, and he asked the guard to bring the monk inside so that he could scold him.

"Why are you behaving like an idiot? I am the king of this country. I am the owner of this palace, this throne, and this crown. Why do you call me a tenant?" the king shouted, shivering with anger. His ego was badly hurt.

"I had come here thirty years ago. There was a different man sitting here. I had come here sixty years ago too. Then again there was a different man sitting here on this throne. If you are the owner of this throne, why do I find different people sitting here at different times?" the old monk asked calmly.

"Well, they were my father and my grandfather." Now the king was a little careful about what he was speaking. This monk didn't seem to him that stupid now.

"They also said they were owners of this throne. Where are they now?" the monk threw another verbal punch at him.

"Well, they are . . . dead," the king replied and started getting the message.

"Good answer. Now maybe you understand why I called you a tenant. Tenants come and ago. Only owners stay permanently," the monk spoke with affection. After this dialogue, the arrogance of the king vanished. He got down from his throne and touched the feet of the monk who didn't seem to be an ordinary man to him now.

Well, we all are tenants but we have started believing that we are the owners. This belief hasn't done us any good. We have developed excessive attachments to things we don't own and would never be able to own. But what's the cure for these pain-in-the-neck attachments? The answer: a strong awareness of death.

The knowledge of our mortality brings a strong detachment in us. When we hear the word 'detachment', many of us start getting a very negative and uncomfortable feeling about it. For us, a detached person means somebody who doesn't care about anything and anybody, who is not affected by the pains of anybody else, and who stays aloof in his own world. The trait which exhibits these habits is not called detachment; it's called indifference. So, if a doctor doesn't care about his patients, he will be called indifferent. But if the same doctor gives the best treatment to a patient without losing his cool over the pain his patient is going through, he will be called detached. Similarly, if a friend doesn't feel the need to help us, he will be called indifferent. And if a friend gives all the help we need without trying to get possessive or jealous, he will be called detached. If a leader doesn't try to understand the problem of his followers, this means he is indifferent. On the other hand, if a leader tries his best to solve the problems of his followers without seeking unnecessary power over them, this means he is detached.

As we see, indifference is full of passive cruelty while detachment is full of silent compassion. Detachment brings a very joyful lightness to our life and also helps us to get rid of unproductive emotional burdens we have been carrying on our shoulders. It lets us take off the heavy clothes of attachments before we plunge into the beautiful ocean of life to swim.

Another problem with attachment is that it makes us expect the things we like to be permanent. In contrast, detachment makes us accept the impermanence of things whether we like them or dislike them. When we are attached to something pleasant, we want it to last forever but when we are detached from things, we know that they would go away one day whether they give us pleasure or displeasure.

This reminds me of a beautiful story that has helped me a lot while going through the highs and lows of life. A rich businessman was dying. He had built his empire from scratch and had gone through lots of ups and downs, profits and losses, and good and hard times before he became successful. While waiting for his last moment, he called his son who was going to inherit his wealth and gave him two rings. He told the son that each ring carried a small piece of paper with a message, and he must read the message of the first ring when his life starts going through very tough times and read the message of the second ring when his life is going through very good times.

Several years passed and a time came when the son's business started facings many setbacks. He was on the verge of bankruptcy and he couldn't see any ray of hope. Then he remembered his father's message and the rings he had given him. He took out the first ring and removed its stone to read the message. The small paper had the following message written over it: 'This too shall pass.' This message gave instant relief to the son. He realised that the hard times won't last forever and his business will come out of the problems with time.

Many years went by again and a time came when the son's business had become so profitable that he became one of the richest people in his country. He was getting accolades and respect from everybody and he was living the life most of us couldn't even dream of. Again, he remembered his father's instruction and the rings he had given. He took out the second ring and removed its stone to read the message. And to his surprise, the small paper had the same message written over it: 'This too shall pass.'

The son understood the wisdom his father wanted to impart. He realised these good times too won't last forever, and his life will always be full of ups and downs. Neither the ups nor the downs are going to be permanent, so it's better not to get too attached to them. This realisation made him calm and peaceful. He was no longer the emotional slave of the various changes which took place in his life.

When we develop an awareness of death, we strongly realise the fact that 'this too shall pass'. We realise that nothing stays forever and that everything has to go away one day. Charlie Chaplin explained this truth succinctly when he said, "Nothing is permanent in this world, not even our goddamn problems."

Years back, I had a very close encounter with death about which I will tell in detail later on in this book. This close encounter taught me that I didn't even own my body and it could go away any day. This realisation didn't turn me into a detached monk on the journey to self-knowledge, but it surely brought a slow and consistent growth of detachment in me towards the sundry elements of life. After this incident, I noticed that I was less affected by the highs and lows of life and the little losses didn't bother me anymore. I felt that my mental peace and inner joy increased in direct proportion with the development of inner detachment. I wish the same benefits to you.

I would like to end this chapter with a funny cartoon I had seen on the internet. I don't know the artist's name otherwise I would have definitely given him the credit here. In the cartoon, a young monk asks an old monk who happens to be his teacher, "Master, can I use emails?"

The teacher replies, "Yes, but it shouldn't have attachments."

Since we are not the monk of that cartoon, we can use as many attachments in our emails as we wish. But we can surely reduce the number of attachments we have in our life with the help of the awareness of death to make our days more joyful and peaceful.

Now we are ready to understand why it's wrong to keep waiting for the right conditions to be happy.

Chapter 27

DISCOVERING THE DELIVERY DATE
OF HAPPINESS

*"God surely did not create us, and cause us
to live, with the sole end of wishing always to
die. I believe, in my heart, we were intended
to prize life and enjoy it, so long as we retain
it. Existence never was originally meant to be
that useless, blank, pale, slow-trailing thing it
often becomes to many, and is becoming to me,
among the rest."*

— Charlotte Brontë, *Shirley*

*Y*ears back, I used to work in an advertising agency in
Delhi that was handling the advertising account of a cold
drink brand. One Saturday I had to go to a blind school
where a small film for the cold drink was to be shot. Going
to the blind school was a new experience that taught me so
many things about blind people.

It was impressive to see how adeptly they were living
a life which was full of difficulties. I also came to know
about the technological innovations which let them use
computers and cellphones. One of the teachers told me the
background stories of many students who were studying
there and teachers who were working there. It was nice
to know about people who had devoted their lives to the

service of blind people without expecting any materialistic benefits in return. But there was one blind girl who attracted everybody's attention. She was very chirpy and couldn't stop joking with the shooting crew members. She knew most of the popular Hindi movie songs which she kept humming all the time. She also challenged the crew members to defeat her in *antaakshari* (an Indian game based on songs). She was one of the happiest and most enthusiastic people I had come across in my life.

I was curious to know about that girl and asked the teacher about her. The teacher told me that the girl was found at the age of six months along with her twin blind brother at the doorsteps of the principal of the blind school. Since then, she has lived in this school with all other students. I asked the teacher if that girl had a special reason to be so happy that day. She said the girl was happy most of the days and rarely complained about anything in her life.

On Monday, I came back to my office and started chit-chatting with my colleagues. Our conversation started with the complaints about coming to the office on Monday. Then our complaints took new directions as people started cribbing about others getting paid more, not getting enough increments, the rising prices at fancy restaurants, traffic jams they had to face in their AC cars, etc. I used to have such conversations every day but that day, they made me compare the situation of that girl with ours.

That girl was born blind, was abandoned by her parents, had lived all her life in a blind school, and would never be able to witness the physical beauty of the world. In contrast, we had loving parents, were physically healthy, earned enough to live a comfortable life, and had the opportunity to see the beauty of the world. But she was happier than us. And though her blindness stopped her from seeing the world, she could see the many reasons to be happy in life. We could see the world but our blindness stopped us from seeing the reasons to be happy. From this, we can conclude that there are two kinds of blind people in this world.

There was one more difference between the blind girl and us. She was unable to cure her type of blindness, but we have the power to cure our blindness with a little change in our attitude. Let me share another story to explain what we need to change.

A renowned Indian spiritual guru had journeyed to learn yoga from a Himalayan yogi when he was very young. The Himalayan yogi promised him that if he stayed there for a few weeks, showed patience, and did everything he was asked to do, the yogi will teach him the secret of a great yogic power. The young man was definitely tempted by this offer. He stayed with the yogi, performed every duty, and when the time period elapsed, he asked the yogi to teach him the secret of the promised yogic power. The yogi smiled and said, "You have worked hard and definitely, you deserve the reward."

The young man's breathing became faster. The expectation of the reward was making him excited. Then the yogi said, "Son, I want to teach you only one thing. Stay happy in life no matter what kind of circumstances you are facing. To be happy, you just need a strong intention and a little effort. That's it."

After listening to this statement, the young man felt as if he had been cheated and his hard work didn't amount to anything. He was expecting some kind of miraculous power, but what he got was a simple and apparently ordinary teaching. But years later, after seeing the ups and downs of life, the young man realised that this was the best teaching he had ever received. In other words, he had developed the same eyes with which that blind girl used to see the world. He had inculcated the ability to find reasons to be happy in the most adverse circumstances.

But most of us behave differently. We have the habit of expecting happiness in some future moment. We put so many conditions on it and convince ourselves that we will be happy only when those conditions are fulfilled. And what happens when some or all of those conditions are fulfilled? We enjoy the happiness for some time and then we come up with another set of conditions which postpone our happiness to another distant day and time.

But when we realise that every day, we are getting one day closer to the end of our life, we understand that it's foolish and impractical to postpone our happiness. If we keep waiting for those ideal conditions to be happy, we might have to wait forever. We understand that if we have put conditions on ourselves to be happy in future, we are the ones who can remove those conditions so that we can be happy right now. Remember that we cannot afford to wait till tomorrow to enjoy life.

To be happy, we don't need lots of conditions; we only need the right intention. I see moments of happiness as coins. Just like a child can fill up his piggy bank by putting a few coins every day, in the same way, we can fill up our life with happiness by living and adding moments of happiness every day. If the child stops putting coins and hopes that his piggy bank will automatically fill on some future day just by coming up with some random conditions, his piggy bank will always remain empty. We will also remain unhappy and dissatisfied if we don't collect the happiness which today's moments have to offer.

When I was in school, I had gone to my art teacher to learn drawing and painting from him. I was hoping that he would suggest me to purchase the costliest art material in the market. But he suggested a simple thing, "Don't wait for the art material from top brands before you could draw. Sketch with whatever you have. If you have a piece of coal in your hand, draw something on the floor. If you can draw well with a piece of coal, you can do more wonderful stuff with the best pencils, watercolours, and canvas in the market."

Thus, we should decide to be happy today with whatever we have got. We cannot wait for the best circumstances available in the market of fantasy. Remember that time is passing by fast and we are not getting younger. So, we need to stop wasting time and make sure that we don't postpone the delivery of happiness and joy anymore.

As our next step, we will learn from a woman who lost the most valuable asset of her life and then gained something far more precious.

Chapter 28

AWAKENING OF A GREAT DESIRE TO FIND THE TRUTH

"Death is a stripping away of all that is not you. The secret of life is to 'die before you die' — and find that there is no death."

— Eckhart Tolle

round 2650 years ago, a young woman in India named Kisa Gotami lost her only child. She had nobody in the world except that little boy whom she loved more than her own life. Her sorrow was limitless. When people came to cremate him, she refused to give the dead body to them. More than anything else, she wanted him back. She wanted to hear his laughter again, she wanted to cuddle him affectionately again, and she wanted to kiss him madly again. The people around her stood helplessly and finally told her that there was only one man who could help her. An enlightened master was visiting the nearby village. People told her that he had conquered death and was the only person who could help her. That woman saw a ray of hope and went to him without any delay.

After her arrival, the woman paid her respect to the master and then poured her heart out. The enlightened master listened to her compassionately and then assured her that he could surely bring her child back to life. But there was one condition: she will have to bring a few seeds of mustard from a house where nobody had died before.

The woman couldn't believe that it was so easy and simple to make her child come alive. With lots of hope and enthusiasm, she went to the first house she could find. The people in that house told her that they would be very happy to donate as many mustard seeds as she wanted if it could help her child but they had seen too many deaths in their house. Just a year back, the old mother of the house owner had left the world. But the woman didn't lose her enthusiasm. There were so many houses in the world and she should definitely find one house which fulfilled the criteria.

By the evening, she had visited at least fifty houses. She got the same reply from every house. They were happy to give her seeds but they couldn't assure her that no death had ever occurred in their houses. She finally started getting the message the enlightened master wanted to convey to her. She realised that everybody dies and her child was not an exception. She also wasn't an exception. It's just a matter of time. Somebody will leave before her and somebody will leave after her. The child had given her an important lesson with his untimely death.

She went back to the enlightened master, became her disciple, and started following the path which would lead to her enlightenment. And the name of the master who opened the door to her enlightenment was Gautam Buddha.

Gautam Buddha's life story is not common in any way. He was born as a prince in a small kingdom in present Nepal. After his birth, a famous guru had predicted that he will become a monk after seeing the misery in the world and will go on to become one of the greatest spiritual masters the world has ever seen. This prediction made his father very upset who wanted an heir for his throne who could expand his kingdom. So, he established a small city especially for his son where he couldn't see old, diseased, and dead people. The young prince was kept in an artificial world where everybody was young, healthy, and looked happy. He was kept away from seeing every kind of misery in the world so that he couldn't develop an attitude of renunciation and become a monk.

But one night, the prince was coming from a festival and he saw an old man, a diseased man, and a dead person. It brought him face to face with the bitter reality of human life. He realised that one day, he would also grow old and sick and death will come to him for sure. He understood that everybody he loved will also meet death one day. Then he saw a monk sitting in meditation and searching for the inner truth. This made the prince feel a strong urge to start the pursuit of the truth. That night, the young prince left his luxurious life, became a monk, and focussed all his energy on the path which led to enlightenment. After six years of intense meditation, he became enlightened and spent the remaining thirty-five years of his life teaching the path of enlightenment to people.

Kisa Gotami and Gautam Buddha felt a strong awareness of death in different ways. The first one had to go through the sorrow caused by the death of her son while Gautam Buddha felt this awareness just by seeing the corpse of a stranger. But the end result was the same. They both found themselves face to face with the question which we all have faced at least once in our lifetime whenever we saw the demise of somebody we knew and loved. Is this physical life the only reality in the world? What will happen to us after our death? Shall we exist in some or other way after it or not?

Most of us try our best to ignore this question so that we can 'move on' in life. But the question comes back to haunt us again and again. It's a stubborn question and it won't stop poking us till the last moment we spend in this world. The good news is that this question carries the seed of a new journey which can lead us to divine bliss and the knowledge of our immortality. This can be compared to how a minor disease can warn us and motivate us to look for ways to find and maintain good health. We just have to make sure that we keep nourishing this question with frequent attention so that it transforms into a burning obsession.

If we look at history, we will find that many people have felt the intensity of this question and have acted upon it. They refused to blindly believe that life ends when we die. They decided to find out what exists after death and why we face so much sorrow in the world. All religions have been founded by great masters who made a firm determination that they will find the answers and, after finding the answer, they helped others find the answer too. It's true that today a major part of many religions has become a tool of exploitation and seeking power over others. But that was not the case when the founders of these religions were alive. If our desire is intense and our intention is pure like theirs, we can also find the answers like them whether we have faith in these religions or not.

This subject reminds me of a beautiful story of a very young boy which is told in an ancient Hindu scripture, Kathopanishad. He was the son of a king who was performing a huge prayer ceremony to please the gods. That king was a miser and he was donating old and useless cows to priests to earn good merit. The boy saw this hypocrisy and asked his father if he would like to donate his son to somebody. After all, a true donation means donating something you love the most, and a father loves his children the most. The son's question irritated his father and he said angrily that he was donating his son to Yamaraja, the god of death. The son being an obedient child quickly started his journey to the place where Yamaraja lived. When he reached Yamaraja's palace, the gatekeeper told him that he had gone somewhere for a few days and the boy will have to wait for his return. The boy waited for three days and three nights. When Yamaraja came back, he was very impressed with the boy's courage and persistence. He asked the boy to ask for three boons from him as compensation for the three days he had spent waiting for the host. The young boy's third boon contained the question regarding death. He wanted to know if there is something which exists after death or not, and if something exists, what does it look like?

Yamaraja was taken aback by this question that came from a young boy. He tried to offer him a huge kingdom, power, and sensual pleasures so that he could deviate from his demand. But the boy said that he didn't see any attraction in the materialistic things Yamaraja was offering because they will also end with his death which will come one day for sure. When Yamaraja saw that the boy's determination was unshakable and his desire to know the truth was like a rock, he gave the boy the answer he wanted. This boy's name was Nachiketa and the story's name is Kathopanishad.

We all have a Nachiketa inside us who doesn't try to ignore or run away from the question of death. That part of us wants to confront death just like the young boy who went to meet Yamaraj fearlessly. It wants answers and it won't stop until it finds out what lies beyond this physical body. We just have to keep this inquisitive and truth-seeking child in us alive.

Our journey towards the truth can start with a small step. We can begin by keeping half an hour aside every day for meditation which is the simplest and most effective way to start this search. We don't have to believe in any religion, dogma, god, or any supernatural deity to get the benefits of this spiritual practice. It's available and beneficial to both theists and atheists. One of the oldest and most helpful meditation techniques is called Vipassana which helped Gautam Buddha become enlightened, and in the last 2500 years, it has helped thousands of people find their real self. You can read about the basic technique in the chapter 'Watch Your Breath' in the next part of the book. You can try this technique and other various methods of your choice to find the one that suits you the best.

The journey to find the real self is very long, but we will start seeing some basic benefits of the meditation practice from the first month itself. We will see that our mind has become quieter, we have become more peaceful, our ability to work has increased, and we can sleep better. The best part of this pursuit is that we don't need anybody or anything to practice meditation regularly. A corner at home, a meditation mat, and a little discipline are all we need.

If we keep seeking and we don't stop, one day a path will open which will take us to the answer to the most important question which arises in us: Who am I?

Part 4

TOOLS

"There's nothing an artist needs more—even more than excellent tools and stamina—than a deadline."
— Adriana Trigiani

I

Build a New Way of Thinking

*I*n ancient India, a guru had a student who was infamous for his stupidity. He was incapable of learning anything new. The guru had tried every method to upload some knowledge into his brain, but every time the student crashed like a bad website. The student also couldn't understand why he couldn't learn anything although he used to put as much effort into studies as his peers. But a very small incident turned his life around.

After struggling with his studies for years, one day, the student decided that education was not his cup of tea. So, he said goodbye to his guru and left for his home. While walking towards his village with heavy steps, he felt thirsty and stopped at a well to have some water. While he was pulling water from the well with the help of a bucket tied with a long rope, he noticed something which was going to change his life. He noticed that the part of the stone platform near his feet had developed some deep marks. Those marks were created by the constant friction of the rope. He couldn't believe his eyes. How could something soft like a rope create such deep marks on something as hard as a stone? In a fraction of a second, he learnt something which his school couldn't teach him in all these years. He learnt that repetition and consistent effort are the secrets of learning anything new. If a soft rope could create such marks on a stone, maybe he also could learn the teachings of his guru by making a consistent effort and repeating what was being taught in the class.

So, the student went back to the guru with a strong determination and begged him to take him back into the ashram. This time, he followed the teachings of the rope and made consistent efforts to learn everything in the syllabus by repeating it again and again during self-study. Within a few years, he became the brightest student in his class. Later on, he became a great scholar in Sanskrit and wrote three important books in his lifetime. The name of this student was Varadaraj.

If we want to make a new learning a part of our mind, we need to follow the principle of the rope. We should repeat that learning again and again till it becomes imprinted in our mind and then our behaviour starts getting automatically guided by our new way of thinking. That's why this book is offering some affirmations which are based on the teachings of the awareness of death. It would be a good idea if you can read the affirmations given below every day at least once for at least three months so that you can make the awareness of death and this new way of thinking a strong part of your mind. You can decide to read all of them or choose a few of them which better suit your thinking and priorities. It would be more beneficial if you can read them just before going to sleep because then your subconscious mind will keep working on them while you will be fast asleep.

Let's go through the affirmations:

1. I have very limited time on the earth. Death can come any day from anywhere. I decide to make the best use of this life to live with happiness, purpose, and satisfaction.

2. Life is short. Therefore, it's not good to always live according to the wishes and plans of others. I'm going to find out what I truly want and I'm going to pursue it with a very strong determination.

3. Death will take away everything one day. I will lose everything one day. So, there is no need to be afraid of losing things. This realisation makes me very courageous, and I am going to pursue the aim of my life with infinite bravery and boldness.

4. The fear of death is the greatest fear in the world. I have confronted this fear and I have accepted it. Now other smaller fears don't have any effect on me. Now I feel fearless which gives me mental peace and tranquillity.

5. I have limited days on this earth. There is no point in postponing things I want to do. If I keep waiting for the best time to do things I want, I will keep waiting forever. That's why I make a promise to myself that I will start living the life I want to live from TODAY.

6. People forget the dead very soon. So, I am not going to give extra importance to others' opinion about what I want to do and what I am doing. It's a small life. I am going to live my life according to what I want deeply, and I'm going to give more importance to my own conviction.

7. We all are going to die soon. I see no point in holding grudges and wasting the time of my life in disliking and hating others. I have compassion for everybody. I enjoy the joy and mental peace which I get from my compassionate attitude. I send good wishes to every person and I seek forgiveness from

those whom I have hurt or harmed intentionally or unintentionally.

8. A day will come when I will be gone forever. I would love to create something in this world which will stay here even after I am gone. It can be as small as a simple drawing or it can be as big as a magnum opus. I am going to give my best to my creative self which is seeking an opportunity to do something amazing.

9. We all have come from dust and very soon, we will go back to dust. But we can leave something behind in this world which will add value to others' lives even after we are gone. It can be as simple as a plant that gives flowers and fragrance to people living near it. I am going to leave something valuable behind for sure.

10. Our loved ones will leave us one by one. Or we will leave our loved ones one day. I'm going to give all of them unconditional love and care every day. Love is the biggest priority of my life and loving relationships are one of the most important things for me.

11. I am going to be a great friend to those people who are on their deathbed. I understand their plight because of my own awareness of death. I am going to listen to them with full sincerity and I am going to give them the comfort and strength they need.

12. Life is a series of many present moments which are given to us in a limited amount. If I don't enjoy this moment, I will lose one moment of happiness. If I enjoy this moment, I will add one moment of happiness to my life. Therefore, I live in the present

moment with full intensity so that I could fill my life with happiness.

13. I am determined to get the maximum happiness out of this short and unpredictable life. I focus on what life has given me rather than what life hasn't given me. I feel grateful for every little and big thing I enjoy in this world. I stay away from the habit of complaining and cribbing because it kills happiness.

14. When we came to this earth, we had nothing. When we will leave this earth, we will have nothing. In other words, we own nothing. Whatever life gives to us is a gift. I take care of everything life gives to me but I also feel detached from all of them. I enjoy the freedom this detachment gives me.

15. We don't know what will happen tomorrow. So, I focus on making my today full of happiness and meaningfulness. A happy today gives a better possibility for a happy tomorrow.

16. Death will take away everything. But is there something in us which lasts even after our death? That's the most important question of my life. That's the biggest search of my life. I am determined to find my real self which is beyond this physical body. I am making a pledge to myself that I will find the ultimate truth. I will keep persisting in my spiritual quest till I find out who I am.

These are some affirmations based on the suggestions in the book. But you can come up with your own affirmations which will come out from an awareness of death you have developed. Whether you follow the affirmations which are given here or write down your own affirmations, what's important is that you read them every day and repeat them hundreds of times over many months so that they become a part of your subconscious mind. You can also record them on your phone and listen to them while doing some work or going to sleep. Remember that the keyword here is repetition. The more you do it, the more benefit you will get out of them.

These affirmations will also work as a compass and give a direction to your life. It's so easy to lose the awareness of death we have developed because of the activities and distractions of life. It's so difficult to maintain the awareness of death because we live in a society where giving attention to the possibility of one's own death is not the top priority of people. We live among people who think they are never going to die and live without any consciousness of their mortality. In such a case, it becomes very important that we create a mental space for ourselves where we can go and strengthen our awareness of death and make sure that we are on the right track to live with the right purpose, motivation, and conviction. These affirmations can be a big help in this direction. Giving them a few minutes every day is enough to reap their benefits.

It can be beneficial to follow these guidelines while working on these affirmations:

1. If you choose to write down your own affirmations, you should write them in the present tense. You should use the simplest language possible and use any language you are comfortable with. They work best with the language in which you think.

2. You should read them at least once a day. If you have enough time, you can read them many times a day. It will make them more effective.

3. If you read them before going to sleep, it will be very effective. As discussed before, the subconscious mind will keep working on them the whole night. It will make your progress much faster. You can also read them just after waking up in the morning. That's the second-best time. If you can read them both before going to sleep and after waking up in the morning, that would be simply wonderful.

4. While reading them, you should give them full concentration. Reading aloud is great. Reading silently with full concentration is even better.

5. You can write these affirmations in a note app on your mobile phone so that they are accessible at any time. I use Evernote app which is very user-friendly. Its free version is enough for our needs. You can download it from Google Play Store.

6. You can also record these affirmations and play them in the background while working or while going to sleep. Even if you don't listen to them attentively, your subconscious mind will keep absorbing them. It would be great if you can put some soothing music in the background along with these affirmations.

7. You should make a pledge that you will listen to these affirmations every day for at least three months. Repetition is the key to success in affirmations. After completing three months, you can continue listening to them for more benefits.

8. It's completely okay to add, remove, or rewrite the affirmations as your understanding develops. There is always a scope for improvement.

9. Reading affirmations gives stronger benefits if you feel positive emotions and conviction during the process. You shouldn't read them as if you are reading some laundry list. You should read them like you are giving a motivational speech to yourself.

10. It's helpful if you keep your affirmations to yourself and share them with only those people who are on the same path. Sharing them with random people might invite escapism or ridicule from them which can be counterproductive.

Before we end this chapter, let's deal with the most important question: What's the best day to start with these affirmations?

The answer is TODAY.

II

Visualise Your Cremation

We have discussed many tools to develop an awareness of death and reap its benefits in the book. For the readers' convenience, those exercises are provided separately in this section. You can quickly refer to them here whenever you get time to practice.

This exercise will use your imagination to create a mental scenario where you can experience your death and learn from it.

1. Go to a place where nobody can disturb you for an hour. Your bedroom will be fine. Switch off your phone so that there is no disturbance.

2. Lie down in a bed or sit in a comfortable chair. Take a few slow and deep breaths.

3. Close your eyes. Imagine that you are dead. Your dead body is lying in a coffin or on a funeral pyre. Feel the deadness in every part of your body. You cannot move any body part. You cannot speak. You cannot open your eyes. You cannot make even the slightest movement. After all, you are dead.

4. It might take some time to feel this emotion in its totality when you are doing it for the first time. But don't worry. Most probably, in less than half an hour, you will start getting the feel of being dead.

5. Visualise your family members, friends, and others surrounding your body. On your metal screen, see their reactions. See their facial expressions. They must be very sad.

6. Feel that this is your last hour on the earth. Very soon your body will be burnt or it will be buried inside the earth. Then your body will turn into ashes or soil. The body you have nourished and decorated for years will become dust.

7. How do you feel now? Let the emotions come up naturally. Don't try to stop or control them. If you feel like weeping, weep. If you feel like shouting, shout. If you feel like lying down quietly, just lie down quietly.

8. Stay in this situation for at least half an hour. Let the experience become as real as it can. This visualisation experience needs some bravery. You are confronting the biggest fear of humankind. You deserve appreciation for taking this step.

9. After lying down for half an hour or more, get up and wash your face. You have taken the first step towards developing awareness of death. Congratulations!

10. If you wish, you can write down your experiences and feelings in a journal. You can evaluate the life you have lived so far. You can ask yourself questions regarding your life and write down the answers. For example, what was the most important thing for you at the moment of death?

11. If you wish, you can do this exercise again to strengthen your awareness. You can choose to do this once a week or once a month for faster progress.

III

VISIT A CREMATION GROUND

If death is the greatest silent teacher in the world, cremation grounds are the best universities on the planet. We should make time to spend a few hours in a cremation ground regularly so that we can develop an awareness of death and contemplate the way we are living our life.

1. Keep a holiday free so that you can spend a few hours at a cremation ground or a cemetery.

2. After going there, you can switch off your mobile or put it on silent mode so that you don't get interrupted.

3. Just sit and watch a dead body being burnt. Or watch the graves under which the dead people are lying quietly.

4. Let the thoughts and feelings come to you. If seeing death arouses feelings of fear, discomfort, and worry in you, then let those feelings come to you. You are confronting the greatest fear of mankind, and it might not be a pleasant journey in the beginning. Give yourself a pat for taking this courageous step.

5. Think about the people who are no more. Think about the people who made their last journey to this place. Think about their lives. Understand that sooner or later, you will also reach this place in a

coffin or a bamboo cot. Let the awareness of death arise in you and grow stronger.

6. You can choose to visit this place again and again, maybe once a month or once a year. The more you visit, the more awareness of death you will develop.

7. Share the details of your visits only with those people who can understand your journey. If you share these details with random people, you might invite negative comments and reactions from people who don't understand your journey.

8. Write your experiences and thoughts in a journal. You can also make notes while sitting there. They will be helpful in your journey to develop the desired awareness.

IV

One-Minute Awareness Pills

*M*any times, whenever we get a few spare minutes, we end up worrying or fantasising about the future. We can change our attitude and utilise those minutes to develop an awareness of death.

1. You can do this exercise whenever you get some free time. Maybe when you are stuck at a red light, when you are waiting for somebody, or when you are walking to someplace.

2. Make a quick mental picture of your funeral. See your dead body on the mental screen.

3. Try to feel how short this life is. Let the realisation that your time in this world is limited come to you.

4. Do it again and again whenever you get a spare minute.

5. Let the awareness of death grow into your mind minute by minute.

V

REMEMBER THE LOVED ONES YOU HAVE LOST

We all have lost at least one person whom we loved immensely. Every person, who leaves the world, leaves a lesson for us. Let their death enhance our awareness.

1. Whenever you get some quiet time, think about a loved one who has left the world.

2. Let the memory of that person come to you. If that memory makes you feel sad, be open to that feeling of sadness. Don't try to run away from it.

3. Remember the wonderful time you enjoyed with that person.

4. Remind yourself that you cannot have the same wonderful time again even if you are the richest and most powerful person on the earth.

5. Realise that one day you too will leave this world as your loved one has left. Let the awareness of death grow in your mind.

6. Realise that the person you loved has left a lesson for you. He or she has taught that nobody is immortal. You are not immortal. Let that lesson go deep into your mind.

7. Send some loving thoughts to the consciousness of that person. Express your gratitude for giving you the lesson.

8. Let the awareness of death motivate you to love those people even more who are alive. Let the awareness of death make you live deeply and evaluate your way of living.

VI

LEARN FROM STRANGER TEACHERS

*E*very day, hundreds of people die in the world due to various reasons. Though we don't know them, we can learn from them.

1. Read the newspapers. Watch the news channels. Read history or watch documentaries on history. They are full of information about people who had an untimely death.

2. Whenever you see or read news about death, don't skip it. Spend a few minutes with it. Think about the people who died. Till a day back, they were living a life like yours. They had plans and aspirations like you. They thought they were going to live for many years.

3. Contemplate how death can come anytime to anybody from anywhere. We all are equally vulnerable to death.

4. If possible, make a folder of news items related to death in your smartphone or computer. You can also maintain a file of newspaper cuttings related to death. Going through that folder or file regularly can nourish your awareness of death.

5. Let those strangers teach you that we should always keep our death in mind because one day it will come to us as well for sure.

VII

FIND SOME CO-TRAVELLERS

The journey towards the awareness of death can be lonely and tiresome in a world where most people seem to assume that they are going to live forever. It would be great to find some like-minded people who can travel with us.

1. Finding people who are open to developing an awareness of death can be tough. Start this search by accepting this fact.

2. Start talking about death and its inevitability with people you come across in daily life. Most of them will become silent, ignore the subject, accuse you of being negative, or change the topic. That's okay.

3. Once in a while, somebody will show interest in what you are talking about. Treasure such people. They are going to be your co-travellers. Discuss the subject with them.

4. You can go to workshops and meditation courses on the subject of death. You can find like-minded people there.

VIII

Build a Mental Monastery

$\mathcal{B}$ooks can always be our great friends. They impart the knowledge and experiences of those who have walked the path before us. They can also create a monastery-like atmosphere for us where we can be focussed on developing an awareness of death.

1. Many insightful books have been written on the awareness of death by people who have spent time with dying people or experienced their own death in some or the other way. Build a bookshelf with such books.

2. Take refuge in these books whenever you get free time from the responsibilities of daily life.

3. These books will create a mental atmosphere for you where you can learn from the experiences of others, develop an awareness of death, and keep yourself safe from the distractions of a world which is too busy to think about death.

4. You can find the names of some of such books in the 'Recommended Readings' section at the end of the book.

IX

WRITE YOUR WILL

We can truly evaluate how well we have lived only on the last day of our life. But we don't have to wait till the last day to evaluate our life. We can write our will by imagining that we have reached the end of life and get very insightful results.

1. Assume that this is the last day of your life. Your time is up. Let the awareness of death become strong.

2. Take one or two hours off from daily life and write your will. Write down how your money and stuff should be distributed among people.

3. Write down the things which made you happy and the things which made you unhappy in the life you have lived so far.

4. If you get a chance to live your life again, what are the changes you would like to make? Describe.

5. What are the things which matter to you most at this time when your life is over? Think it over and write it down.

6. What are the suggestions you would like to give to the people who will be left behind?

7. You can use this will as a guideline to live your life. It will help you choose the correct priorities in the years to come. It will also strengthen your awareness of death.

X

FIND OUT THE MOST IMPORTANT THINGS

*W*hen somebody asked a sculptor how he created beautiful statues from rocks, he gave a simple reply, "I take my chisel and remove everything from the rock which is not a part of the statue." If we want to create a beautiful life from the earthly existence we are given, we need to pick up the chisel of the awareness of death and remove everything from our life which is not truly important.

1. Take a piece of paper and answer these questions:

   - What's the most important thing I would like to do if I had *one day* to live?
   - What's the most important thing I would like to do if I had *one month* to live?
   - What's the most important thing I would like to do if I had *one year* to live?
   - What's the most important thing I would like to do if I had *ten years* to live?

2. It would be easier to find the correct answers if you visualise your death and feel how short your life is.

3. It's not important to get all the answers in a single sitting. You might need a week or a month or a year or

many years to get the correct answers. Your answers might also change with time. The good thing about this exercise is that you have started the process of finding out what's truly important for you.

4. Once you find out the most important things of your life, you can start making time for them and ignore the things which don't matter much to you.

We can use a litmus test to find out what matters most to us when we are stuck between two or more things to choose from.

Suppose you have got two or more options and you have to make a quick decision to choose the best one. Ask yourself which option you would prefer to choose if you had only one year or one month or one day to live. The most important one will automatically emerge and grab your attention. For example, you have to choose between two ideas for your business. You can ask yourself which idea you would prefer to work on if you had only one year to live. You will get a direct insight into the correct answer.

XI

WRITE YOUR OBITUARY

*A*lfred Nobel's attitude towards his life changed completely when he read his obituary which was printed by mistake. In that obituary, he was called a 'merchant of death' because he had invented and sold dynamite. He decided to change his life by donating most of his money and starting a prize that would be given to the biggest contributors to the evolution of mankind. We can also take a tip from his life to make significant changes in the way we live.

1. Take a piece of paper and write down your obituary. Look at your life from the eyes of a third person and see how you would be remembered after your demise.

2. Take help from your friends. Ask them to write your obituary. Find out how they would remember you. What are the most unforgettable qualities you have which they find worth remembering?

3. This imaginary obituary can give you insights into how you are living and what changes you must make in your life.

4. Start changing your life till it starts matching the ideal obituary you want to be written for you.

XII

HELP THE DYING WITH LISTENING AND TONGLEN MEDITATION

*P*eople on their deathbeds go through immense mental and emotional suffering. They are surrounded by people who don't want to accept the fact that it's time for them to leave. They find it tough to share their pent-up emotions and thoughts with others. If we have developed an awareness of death, we can understand their plight and be very helpful to them by doing these two things.

First, you can listen to them compassionately.

1. Most probably that person knows that he or she doesn't have much time left on this planet. Medicines and doctors can only delay the departure a bit.

2. You don't have to give them the bad news. Just sit with them with your full presence. Ask questions about how they are feeling.

3. Your goal should be to listen to them with full acceptance of their plight. They would want to share their emotions and thoughts. Without passing any judgement or giving opinions, just listen to them with compassion.

4. Let them share whatever they want. Let them feel peaceful and light by helping them share everything

with you. You can keep watching your breath to stay calm and present.

5. Your compassionate listening can be the most valuable gift they would need in this tough time. Don't shy away from giving it.

Second, you can practice a meditation method called Tonglen to reduce their suffering. It can be practised while sitting with them or even if you are far away from them at some other place. The technique is very simple.

STEP 1: Sit or lie quietly and get comfortable. Start taking many slow and deep breaths. It will make you relaxed and calm.

STEP 2: Close your eyes. Imagine the person that you want to help. It can be the person on the deathbed. It can also be the person who has already died. Or it can also be the person who is going through some other kind of pain. Focus on that person and on their struggle and feel their pain.

STEP 3: Take a deep breath, slowly. Focus on their negative energy and things that trouble them. Imagine yourself breathing in their pain and suffering. You can also visualise their pain in the form of black smoke which you are taking inside. Visualise that as the black smoke is leaving their body and entering your nostrils, they are feeling peaceful and relaxed.

STEP 4: Breathe out. As you breathe out, imagine that white smoke is coming out of your nose and entering their body. That white smoke contains peace and joy.

Imagine that the white smoke is filling their body with comfort and happiness.

STEP 5: Repeat. Continue this practice of breathing in pain and breathing out peace over and over again for many minutes. You can also do it for half an hour or more, several times a day.

You can also teach this technique to the dying person if they are open to it. It will help them a lot on an emotional and spiritual level.

To learn more about Tonglen, you can refer to these two books:

1. *The Tibetan Book of Living and Dying* by Sogyal Rinpoche

2. *When Things Fall Apart: Heart Advice for Difficult Times* by Pema Chodron

XIII

BE TOTALLY PRESENT

*W*henever a loved one passes away, many times we feel that we didn't spend enough time with that person. The bad news is that we cannot control how much time we get to spend with that person. After all, life is short and unpredictable. The good news is that we can decide to get the most out of whatever time we get to spend with that person. It just takes a little effort to do that.

1. Whenever we spend time with a loved one, usually we are distracted by too many things. We are daydreaming or checking our phone or thinking about what to say in reply. These distractions steal the beauty of our interaction.

2. Make a firm determination that you are going to be fully present with a person for certain time duration, maybe twenty minutes.

3. Switch off your mobile or put it on silent mode. Take a silent pledge that you are going to be fully present with that person.

4. Focus on everything that person says. It doesn't mean you have to stare into his or her eyes. Just be comfortable. You can also watch your breath. It will bring you in the present moment.

5. Instead of getting attention from that person, try to give full attention to him or her. Assume that the person is the most important person in the world right now. Listen to him or her with full sincerity. If your mind wanders away to something else, bring it back to their words. Feel the sensation of being fully present in your entire body.

6. Feel the difference in that person's response towards you. If you are fully present, that person will feel more comfortable with you and talk more uninhibitedly. You will feel a growing intimacy between both of you. You might also get a compliment from him or her for your changed behaviour.

7. You can apply this principle with every person you interact with. You will start noticing an amazing difference in your relationships.

XIV

WATCH YOUR BREATH

$\mathcal{M}$editation is probably the best way to learn how to be in the present moment and gain mental calmness. If the awareness of death leads us to the desire to know the ultimate truth beyond our physical reality, meditation can act as a very helpful tool in this direction. Here I want to share my understanding and experience of the meditation technique I have been practising for years. It would be great if you would want to try it and find out if it benefits you.

Breath is the most important part of life. We start breathing from the moment we are born, and we keep breathing till the moment our body dies. Breath is available to everybody. Breath doesn't belong to any religion, faith, caste, creed, race, or a particular community. This meditation technique is related to the activity of breathing.

Let's do a small experiment right now.

1. Set the timer for five minutes on your cellphone. Then sit in a comfortable position on a chair, on a bed, or on the floor. It hardly matters where you sit as long as you feel comfortable and don't feel the need to make any movement.

2. Close your eyes and bring your focus on your nose and start observing your breathing. When the air goes in, watch it. When the air goes out, watch it. You

don't have to make any changes to your breathing. You just have to watch its natural course.

3. If you find it difficult to recognise the movements of your breath, then you can watch the sensation in your nostrils due to the passing of air. When the air goes in, you will feel a cool sensation in the nostrils. When the air goes out, you will feel a warm sensation in the nostrils.

4. If you find it difficult to notice the sensations, you can then focus on the movement of your belly. As you breathe in, your belly will rise. As you breathe out, your belly will fall flat.

5. Initially, you might find that your breathing is a little rough or turbulent. But after a few minutes of watching the breath, you will notice that your breathing is becoming calmer and slower. As the breathing becomes calm and slow, you will notice that your mind also starts becoming peaceful. If you enjoy this experience, you can continue watching your breath even after the timer completes five minutes.

This little experience carries the basic principle of one of the oldest and most effective meditation techniques ever practised in the history of humanity. It also shows that our mental and emotional state is directly linked to our breathing. When our breathing starts becoming calm, our mental and emotional state also starts becoming calm. And the most effective way to make our breathing calm is to watch it. We don't have to do anything to make our breathing calm; we just have to watch it. The following example explains this. If we take a glass of water and shake it a bit, the water inside it will become turbulent. If we want to make the water still, we just need to leave it there without any interference. Within a few minutes, the water will start becoming still on its own. Similarly, our breathing also becomes calm if we watch it without making any interference, which automatically leads to a calmer mind.

Now we can expand our experiment to other parts of our life. Whenever you feel angry, agitated, or worried, you will notice that your breathing pattern is turbulent and rough. As we discussed a little ago, our mental and emotional state is directly linked to our breathing. Therefore, in such a situation, you can start watching your breath to calm yourself and bring mental peace.

Now it's time to convert this little experiment into a regular meditation practice:

1. If you can keep a corner in your home especially for meditation, it would be very beneficial. If you don't have so much space at your home, you can meditate on your bed or a chair. You can sit cross-legged or you can sit normally on a chair. Choose the position which is comfortable with you.

2. It would be ideal if you can meditate for thirty minutes in the morning and thirty minutes in the evening or night. But if you cannot get so much time, try to give at least ten minutes in the morning and ten minutes in the evening. It would be great if you can meditate as the first thing after getting up and as the last thing before you go to sleep. After seeing the benefits, you might want to increase the duration of meditation on your own.

3. Set the timer for the duration you have chosen. Sit in a comfortable position. Make sure there is no discomfort in any part of the body. Make sure you sit with a straight spine. Now close your eyes and start watching your breath. Watch its natural course. Don't try to make any changes to it.

4. If you start feeling that you cannot watch your breath for more than a few seconds and your mind starts wandering away, then congratulations to you. It means that you are on the right path. It means that you can see how turbulent our minds are. It's a sign of progress in the right direction.

5. Whenever your mind starts wandering, bring it back to the breath. If it wanders away a hundred times, bring it back to the breath a hundred times. It's that simple.

6. As you keep watching your breath, you will realise that it starts becoming calm. And as you experienced earlier in the experiment, your mind will also start becoming calm.

After a few days of practice, you will notice that your mind has started staying calm during the daytime when you are not meditating. You will also start seeing the benefits of meditation in other aspects of your life. Now you might feel motivated to make your meditation practice more regular. You will also notice after a few days or weeks that now you can sleep better. Watching your breath before going to sleep is way more beneficial than surfing the net or watching a movie. Your sleep will carry the calmness and peace generated by the meditation into your mind.

That's the basic process of this meditation technique. It's called Vipassana or Anapana and it has been mentioned in many ancient spiritual scriptures of India. Around 2500 years ago, it was rediscovered by the Buddha who practised it to become enlightened. Then he kept teaching it to his followers so that they could get the benefits of this meditation. Since then, it has been practised by millions of people in various countries and millions of people are still practising it.

As you might have noticed that we don't need to become a Buddhist or Hindu to practice this technique. You can be an atheist and still practice it without making a change in your beliefs. This meditation technique doesn't cost any money or costly props. You can practice it anywhere and anytime.

I would like to share a few more things to make your practice stronger:

1. You can practice this meditation while sitting, walking, lying down, or doing something else. You just need to make sure that you are watching your breath. You can also watch your breath while keeping your eyes open when you are not sitting in a meditation posture. But it's advisable that you don't skip your morning and evening sitting sessions.

2. You can also do one-minute meditations. It means whenever you get a spare minute, you can watch your twenty to thirty breaths. It will make you calm and improve your concentration.

3. You should try not to skip your sitting sessions even for a single day. If you are too busy on someday, you

can sit for just one session for ten to fifteen minutes. But try to maintain the regularity of your practice.

4. Whenever you feel agitated, angry, or worried, you can watch your breath for five to thirty minutes. It will make you calm and give you mental clarity. It's better than looking for a cigarette, alcohol, or some other intoxicant.

5. While talking to others, you can keep silently watching your breath. It will bring you in the present moment and improve your listening skills. The other person might also feel better while talking to you because of your full presence.

I have shared a very small and basic part of this meditation practice. If you want to learn more about this technique to understand it deeply, you can do these things:

1. You can take a 10-day Vipassana course. It's freely available to those who are ready to give time and effort. For more info on this course, you can visit: www.dhamma.org.

2. If you cannot manage a course, you can take help from some wonderful books on meditation and learn the details of this technique while practising at home. Here are some of the books which I have found immensely helpful:

    i. *Mindfulness in Plain English* by Bhante Henepola Gunaratana
(The contents of this book are freely available here: www.vipassana.com/meditation/mindfulness_ in_plain_english.php)

ii. *The Mind Illuminated: A Complete Meditation Guide Integrating Buddhist Wisdom and Brain Science for Greater Mindfulness* by Culadasa and Matthew Immergut

In case you feel that this meditation technique doesn't suit you, you can try other techniques. But I would suggest that one should give it a regular practice of six months before switching on to some other technique. The goal of every genuine meditation technique is to turn us inwards and make our mind still so that we can experience the deeper realities of ourselves. Watching our breath is one of the simplest and most effective ways to achieve this goal.

Conclusion

"Death is the greatest teacher. Silence is its language. Awareness is the fee we pay to learn from it."

Years back, when I was working in a company, I couldn't help noticing a peculiar work habit among a majority of people. Whenever a new project came or a new assignment was given, for many days they acted as if there's no responsibility on them to deliver the work. They got into action mode only when they got close to the deadline. Basically, they responded only when the pressure of delivery increased and there was no scope to procrastinate the stuff. In other words, the deadline was the only thing that made them feel alive.

This book is a small effort to remind ourselves that life also comes with a deadline. The only difference between my previous workplace and our life is that they used to announce a clear date as the deadline for every work. But when it comes to human life, most of us are not given that date. The deadline can come fifty years later or it can come today. We never know.

There is more to this. Frankly speaking, we all hated deadlines at our workplace. But guess what? Without deadlines, we would have never been able to deliver the work. And without delivering the work, we could never get our salaries because our company used to earn revenue on the basis of the work we delivered. Because of this, I now understand that deadlines are not to be feared or hated. They should be accepted and respected. Deadlines were the reason why we earned well and lived a good life. Deadlines were the alchemy which transformed lazy and procrastinating people into hardworking and goal-oriented professionals.

We possess this kind of alchemy in our life also which can transform us into a focussed person who knows what he wants and who can give his all to achieve what he wants. In this book, we have discussed how to recognise this alchemy, pay respect to it, and make its best use to make our lives more successful, meaningful and joyful. We don't have to wait for a crisis or a life-threatening disease to understand that this alchemy exists. We can develop this awareness today while we are healthy, strong, and full of energy. We can wake up right now to live a purposeful life so that we can go for the long sleep later on with a heart filled with satisfaction and no regrets.

As we saw, this awareness of death can help us find out what we actually want to do in life. We can decide to create masterpieces like Dostoevsky or Steve Jobs or we can decide to pursue enlightenment like the Buddha or we can decide to do something selflessly for the benefit of people like Dashrath Manjhi or we can even live a simple life with the people and things we love. What matters is that whatever we choose to do comes from our inner self and not from societal pressure or desperation to become like everybody else. With the awareness of death, we would act like the batsman who is always conscious that his innings could come to an end at any moment. Only then we would be able to do our best and live a life that gives us inner satisfaction.

It was lovely having a conversation with you on a topic very few people want to talk about. I have shared my thoughts which were based on my experiences, readings, and contemplation. You might agree with some of them and disagree with some of them. But I will feel that the book was successful even if you discard the entire book and take just one thing from it. If you develop even a bit of the awareness of death and if this awareness makes you evaluate the way you are living your life, I will be happy with my effort. And if you already had the awareness of death and it got stronger after reading this book, I will be content with my endeavour.

On a final note, I would like to share a journal entry of an incident from my life in which I had a close encounter with death. This is the most precious event of my life which played a very important role in the way I live and I look at my life today. You can read it in the next section 'My Story'.

My Story
Yesterday Death Kissed Me and Then Ditched Me

"Death is the end of life we are living.
Awareness of death is the beginning of life we
should be living."

Written on 24th April 2011

Just twenty-four hours back I experienced something which may seem scary to some and feels like just a scary dream to me right now. You may call me lucky that I am alive to tell you this story.

Yesterday, on 23 April 2011, I reached Rishikesh with nothing but a small backpack. It was 3:30 a.m. and I knew only one thing that I had to go to Ram Jhula where all the hotels and *dharamshalas* (public resthouse) are located. It was too early and none of them were open. So, I decided to spend one hour on the cemented bank of the Ganges. It was a lovely experience! Cool breeze, calmness, and nothing to enter your ears except the sweet sound of the flowing river. Well, this sweet sound was going to turn into cacophony a few hours later.

I meditated there for one hour. It made me feel like an Indian yogi who had renounced everything and was busy finding the heavenly bliss within him. Then I checked into a hotel, put my stuff there, and started roaming around the small city with a small bag. In the noon, I decided to spend a few hours on the beautiful bank of the river. I could see fluorescent grey sand, shiny rocks, and green water speeding like an army of centipedes. I then sat on a small rock, pulled out my drawing book, and started drawing random stuff. There were families, couples, and sadhus taking a bath with ultimate ease. It brought me some courage and I decided to go into the water. The water was cold. I kept going in and coming out. But I couldn't come out this time. I was enjoying myself waist-deep in the water and took one step ahead, just a small step, ignorant of the huge pit waiting for me.

That step changed the whole quality of the experience. I was fluttering like a caged bird in the water, trying to get my foot on solid ground and keep myself above the surface of the water. It didn't help much since I have never tried my hand at swimming before. I became frustrated, helpless, and confused. Confused because too many thoughts were striking my head: 'What's this happening?' 'Am I dying?' 'No way. I can't be dying. Death is something that happens to others, not to me.' 'Palmistry says I have a strong line of life. Idiots! Now I know palmistry is bullshit.' 'Oh, no! I am going to die. It's death. Pure death. I am here for just a few more seconds.'

Then a blinding white light flashed in my eyes and a final thought came into my head: 'How is my mother going to feel when she comes to know (if she comes to know) that I am gone forever?' Then the light and the thought vanished. I gripped my nose as the final effort to keep myself afloat and lost my consciousness. Have you seen Danny Boyle's movie, *127 Hours?* These 127 seconds were not less intense than those 127 hours the hero had spent with his hand under the rock.

When I came back to my senses, I was lying on the sand like an injured snake. I had a minimal sense of what was going around. Many people had surrounded me. I had to work hard just to open my eyes for a second. I could hear what they were saying for a moment. My entire body was aching. This happens when the amount of Gangajal exceeds the amount of blood in your body. I started vomiting buckets of water. It helped me a lot. I also had a momentary hope that I would be okay in a few minutes with the help of sheer willpower. But sometimes willpower also needs a little help from physical power which I had lost entirely.

What happened in the next one hour is in my memory as short flashes. I remember lying on a motorboat, getting into an ambulance with an oxygen mask on my nose, and being assisted by two people. Later on, I came to know they were Wing Commander Ajay Kishore Mishra and Mr Gaurav Tripathi. Mr Ajay was an Air Force officer to whom I owe the remaining part of my life completely. They took me to a hospital where I was given glucose and more oxygen. Doctors checked my pulse rate and blood pressure and assured me that I was out of any serious danger. Then Ajay called up my father and brother, telling them the entire story. It scared them and worried them. My sister, brother-in-law, and my mother came to know about it. I started getting calls but I was in no condition to receive them.

After one hour of helpless and senseless lying, I finally got some strength to open my eyes. Ajay and Gaurav had left some fruits for me, promising to come back after a few hours. By then, my father, brother, sister, and brother-in-law had gotten their air tickets booked to Delhi. Like many other government hospitals, there was nobody to attend to me except some bodies lying on the beds around me. One old man was lying on the floor. He seemed to be in deep sleep. He was a victim of *nashaakhuranas* (they make the travellers on trains or buses smell some intoxicant and rob them of every paisa they have). He had not opened his eyes for three days. One young man was lying on a bed, badly injured with blood scattered on his head and hands. He was beaten up by some goons. But the cops were interrogating him as if he had beaten up the goons and had gotten himself admitted into the hospital for redemption. The third body belonged to another young man. He had just met with a road accident. The doctors and nurses were discussing when to do his post-mortem.

By evening, I had gained enough strength to walk a little bit. I went to the male toilet. The dirt out there could relieve anybody of his desire to relieve himself. Then Ajay and his brother-in-law, Bohitesh, came to meet me. They told me the entire story as it happened. They saw me beating the water with hands and legs incessantly. At first, they thought I was swimming in an unusual way but quickly they realised that nobody could ever swim that way. Then they saw me gripping my nose with fingers and taking a dive. After a few moments, my body was floating on the water. They quickly reached to me and tried to hold me. It was a dangerous thing to do considering the speed of the water. Ajay tried to hold me from the back. My body was stiff like a wooden block. They started waving their hands to a rafting boat. The man on the boat quickly reached to me. He was wearing a life jacket that could manage weight up to 150 kg. With his help, my senseless body was brought on the sand.

Quickly, people surrounded me. Something interesting to watch, eh! I had lost my pulse and breathing. I looked every inch dead. Some of the onlookers transformed

HOW I WAS SAVED

themselves into medical experts and started giving crisp commentary on why it was useless trying to save me. For five minutes, Ajay and his wife, Vani, kept trying to push my back and give some first aid therapy. Then my stiff body made its first physical movement. I started vomiting water. The holy water of the Ganges had purified me from inside, and now it needed to come out.

As the water came out, my breathing came back. I also started making some sound. It looked like I had chances of staying alive. They got me on a motorboat to cross the river and get to a hospital. The boat was in a nasty mood and its motor broke down in the middle of the river. Another motorboat arrived after a while. I was shifted to it. Ajay and Gaurav were holding my arms. We walked to the ambulance which was one kilometre away. They took the help of a cop who seemed disinterested at first, citing the fact that he was on VIP duty. But after some verbal rebuke, he decided to help. There was another stimulant also for his desire to help. He wanted to know what I was carrying in my bag. Maybe he was hopeful that he would find lots and lots of currency notes of 1,000 rupees. People at the government hospital didn't seem very helpful either. The staff and attendants refused to touch the stretcher. But in the end, I was admitted there.

I have already written what happened in the hospital after that. Ashutosh, a very good friend of my brother, quickly took a taxi from Delhi. He reached there by the night and then together, we departed for Delhi. Right now, I am staying at his house, looking completely healthy. No symptoms of any physical or psychological damage are visible on my body. But I am feeling weak. It will take me one or two days to get my strength back. Ajay and Gaurav have called me up many times asking about improvement in my health.

As the news is spreading, I am getting calls from my relatives. They are asking only one question: "Why the hell did you go alone?" Now I feel I just saw a scary dream. But it was no dream. My destiny had put me into the jaws of death and had snatched me back. You may call it what is known as a near-death experience. I don't remember anything about what happened during those fifteen-twenty minutes when

I had lost my consciousness. I don't remember my soul being pushed into an endless tunnel, seeing weird lights, or meeting any angel who said to me, "Alok, your time is not over yet. Go suffer the world for a few decades more." But I remember the extreme helplessness I felt when I was trying to save myself from drowning. Now I know I am as near to death as anybody else. Death is not impartial to somebody just because he is young, healthy, and slightly cocky about his imaginary omnipotence.

Generally, such incidents bring a permanent shift in the paradigms of people who experience them. They start looking at life in a completely new way. They lose the fear of death, become more loving towards others, and start thinking more about what is really important and unimportant in life. I have experienced no such change in my thinking so far. But I am hopeful. If such a rare experience doesn't bring any valuable change in me, it would stay in my head just as an unforgettable but meaningless event.

Recommended Readings

1. *The Tibetan Book of Living and Dying* by Sogyal Rinpoche

2. *A Dialogue with Death* by Eknath Easwaran

3. *The Nine Contemplations of Atisha* by Joan Halifax Roshi

4. *Dying To Be Me* by Anita Moorjani

5. *The Last Lecture* by Randy Pausch

6. *The Five Invitations: Discovering What Death Can Teach Us* by Frank Ostaseski

7. *Tuesdays with Morrie* by Mitch Albom

8. *The Mind Illuminated: A Complete Meditation Guide Integrating Buddhist Wisdom and Brain Science for Greater Mindfulness* by Culadasa and Matthew Immergu

9. *Mindfulness in Plain English* by Bhante Henepola Gunaratana

10. *The Miracle of Mindfulness* by Thich Nhat Hanh

11. *Main Mrityu Sikhata Hun (Hindi Edition)* by Osho

12. *The Power of Now: A Guide to Spiritual Enlightenment* by Eckhart Tolle

13. *When Things Fall Apart: Heart Advice for Difficult Times* by Pema Chodron

14. *The Deeper Wound: Recovering the Soul from Fear and Suffering* by Deepak Chopra

15. *Advice on Dying: And Living a Better Life* by Dalai Lama

16. *Change Your Thoughts, Change Your Life* by Wayne Dyer

17. *LIFE!: Reflections on Your Journey* by Louise L. Hay

18. *How I Helped My Dad Die* by Esme E. Deprez

19. *Being Mortal* by Atul Gawande

ACKNOWLEDGEMENTS

I am alive to write this book because of Ajay K. Mishra who risked his own life to save mine in Rishikesh. I am eternally grateful to him. I am also thankful to Vani Mishra, Gaurav Tripathi, and Ashutosh Kumar for offering their help during the critical incident.

I express my gratitude to Ashok Chopra, Hay House, for seeing potential in my book and helping with his feedback. I am thankful to Aditya Jarial for wonderfully editing the book.

I am deeply thankful to my parents, Madhuri and Yogendra Bhakta, for providing an atmosphere in which I could write this book for months without any worries. I am also grateful for the support and encouragement of my friends—Rupa Dash, Ajay Sharma, Rashmi Ambastha, Bhavana Gupta, Khusi Pattanayak, and Tushar Chavan. Most importantly, I would like to express my gratitude to my school teacher, Rajesh Kumar Roy, and college professor, Samantak Das, for nourishing the seeds of reading and writing during my student days.

HAY HOUSE INDIA

Look within

Join the conversation about latest products, events, exclusive offers, contests, giveaways and more.

f Hay House India

@HayHouseIndia

@HayHouseIndia

HayHouse.co.in

HealYourLife.com

We'd love to hear from you!

BESTSELLERS

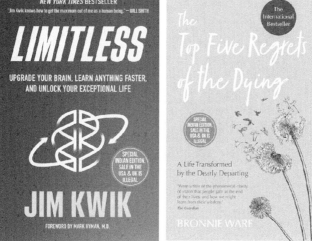

BESTSELLERS